My God

Makes House Calls

My God

Makes House Calls

Nalley T. Osland

iUniverse, Inc.
New York   Bloomington

My God Makes House Calls

The views expressed in this work are solely those of the author and do not necessarily reflect the views of the publisher, and the publisher hereby disclaims any responsibility for them.

iUniverse books may be ordered through booksellers or by contacting:

iUniverse
1663 Liberty Drive
Bloomington, IN 47403
www.iuniverse.com
1-800-Authors (1-800-288-4677)

Because of the dynamic nature of the Internet, any Web addresses or links contained in this book may have changed since publication and may no longer be valid.

ISBN: 978-1-4401-2172-2 (pbk)
ISBN: 978-1-4401-2173-9 (cloth)
ISBN: 978-1-4401-2358-0 (ebook)

Library of Congress Control Number: 2009921499

Printed in the United States of America

iUniverse rev. date: 1/29/2009

This book is dedicated in memory of

My grandfather and writer,

George Thomas Nalley

And

To my friend, husband, and sweetheart,

Stuart Osland

Contents

Foreword

My God Makes House Calls came to me at a crucial time in my life. As I began reading the chapters, they gave me courage to start relying on God for everything. It helped me begin to walk as a Christian and be led by the Holy Spirit.

Brenda B., New York

Nalley Osland opens the door for God to use the power of the true testimony in the lives of those reading her book. The profound southern simplicity in her writing resounds like a non-fictional Faulkner work with the purpose and intent of a woman of wisdom.

Tina Z., Pennsylvania

Acknowledgments

This memoir is about my life entwined with three others. These are my words expressing several years of our lives. I tried unsuccessfully to write this book before, and for various reasons failed. Then one day the words began to flow from my heart to my fingertips. I cannot express adequately my appreciation to every member of the South Carolina Writers Workshop, especially the Lexington, South Carolina, Chapter. They patiently helped me with the critiquing and grooming of this book.

Prologue

As I hurried out the front door Mother shouted, "Don't do it even if everyone else does!"

I was just eight years old and my mother always told me not to take communion, but when I entered the church, it was another world. God and I were there alone. Today, we were told to come down to the beautiful wood altar in front of the church and kneel to receive communion. Usually, we were served the juice and cracker at our seats.

I always obeyed my mother, but her words were not a part of this sacred time. I was led by God's presence: innocently, like the child I was, I followed. This time would be different. I would hear the Lord's voice for the first time.

I solemnly knelt, waiting to be served when I heard a loud metallic sound reverberating, piercing this sacred moment. I was startled, and looked toward the sound. I saw a man in a brown suit kneeling beside me. After being served, he thoughtlessly threw coins down on the altar; just like the movie cowboys did after having their drinks in the saloons. The sound of the coins hitting the wood altar continued to resound in my spirit, and I felt something dreadful had taken place. Then the Lord spoke to me, "You can't buy this!"

A feeling of deep disappointment filled my heart as I gently put the small cup, now empty, on the polished wood altar rail. My time of communion was ruined, mixed with regret, as my mother's words filled my thoughts. "Don't do it, even if they do!" With the negative intrusion, I felt guilt. I had disobeyed my mother.

Then, amid disappointment, I realized the Lord had spoken to me. Remembering his words, removed the tainted action which had taken place, restored his presence reaffirming the sacredness and love of our communion.

Chapter 1

A Desperate Search

I watched Joann pin the pattern for her Easter dress to the blue polka dot material. Earl, her husband, was in the kitchen fixing our seafood supper. They worked well together and I envied them.

"You look nice tonight," Earl said. "I haven't seen you look this good since before you got married. "

I laughed. For some unknown reason, that morning I was happier than I had been in a long time. I never went anywhere without my children but this day, I decided to visit with my cousins while Stuart stayed home with our children.

I had been looking forward to this time. As Joann worked, I began to feel peculiar, like I was sinking down into something unseen. The experience was indescribable. I couldn't understand what was happening. I felt weak and shaky, almost without strength to lift my head.

I rested my head on my arms on the table. "I have to go home."

She stopped working and looked quizzically at me. "Why?"

"I don't feel well."

Earl came out of the kitchen wiping his hands on the dishcloth. "What's the matter? Do you want to lie down? You can go in the bedroom until supper."

I knew they worked hard to make this a special night, and I was sorry to disappoint them. I was frightened and needed Stuart.

"No, I'm sorry but I need to go home. I'm not sick, I can't explain it, but I really feel bad!"

When I stood, I was so weak I wondered whether I could make it home. Earl offered to drive me, but I insisted on going alone. I didn't want to talk.

It was March, 1960. The route home to Thunderbolt, a small town on the edge of Savannah, Georgia, was dark with just a few houses. As I was passing Bonaventure Cemetery with its old oak trees and the wind blowing their wispy hanging moss, the dim lighting distorting the eerie shadows, set the stage for my terror on this narrow winding road. I met one car which gave me some comfort. I was vigilantly watching its lights as we approached each other, and the car just disappeared. It was then; I knew for certain, I was losing my mind. I was so frightened; the beat of my heart shook my body. I sensed my life was in danger and clenched the steering wheel tighter.

When I arrived home, I clumsily struggled with the locked door and rushed to my bedroom falling fully clothed in bed. How could I feel so strange and not be sick? It seemed the foot of my bed was elevated and all the blood was rushing to my head. I had never felt like this in my life. I was terrified. If I had been angry, or depressed, I might have expected something, but nothing like this. The entire day had been wonderful. I even felt normal. I thought, maybe if I cry, whatever is happening will stop! But I couldn't cry, I wasn't sad, nor did I have a reason to be sad. What is wrong with me?

As I calmed down, I could hear the sound of the television coming from the living room. Stuart didn't know I was home. I called to him, but all that came out was a raspy whisper. There wasn't enough air to call out, but he must have heard something because he came to the bedroom and was surprised to find me. I tried to tell him what was happening, but he couldn't hear me. He put his ear close to my lips and was alarmed. He called my doctor.

I don't know what the doctor thought, but he called in a tranquilizer. Although I appreciated medicine, I was wary of drugs. This night was the beginning of time when an overwhelming fear tried to take control of me. Deep within me wondered if I wasn't on the brink of insanity. What was happening to me was beyond my control. I didn't realize it was spiritual and not physical. It is written in the Bible: "For God hath not given us the spirit of fear; but of power, and of love, and of a sound mind."[1]

I hid what was happening so well; even Stuart didn't suspect. When we would go out for a ride or to the store, a foreboding that something bad was going to happen would grip me, and yet, I felt the same sinister feeling at the thought of staying home. No one realized how I felt, and I didn't tell them because they would think I was going crazy.

Stuart was in the Air Force and once in the spring we attended a barbeque with other military families. There were so many people, I felt threatened and wanted to escape. After that time, I avoided crowds whenever possible.

My many medical complaints (which often came in the midnight or early morning hours) were beginning to irritate my doctor. Once, while cleaning my refrigerator, I reached behind and a prong stuck my finger. It hurt. I cleaned and put medicine on it and was busy working because this was in the early part of the day. I went to bed that night, but awoke at 3:00 in the early morning. My finger was throbbing. That fearful anxiety came over me, and I knew I was going to die from Tetanus.

I woke Stuart and he called the doctor. Well, he wasn't delighted, but told Stuart to take me to the emergency room. Then he called and told them the story and that when I arrived at the ER, they were to give me the biggest shot they had. I felt so foolish, but what could I do since I was controlled by this terrible fear?

I worried the medical community would laugh at me but the fear and darkness which plagued me were more than real, and how could they help me if I didn't tell them. On the other hand, how would they treat this condition? Would they put me in a mental institution? Would I be put on strong medication or even suffer shock treatments? I had seen people in these circumstances, and I was deathly afraid.

My mother could tell something was wrong and she told me, "You better get control of yourself." That was the only advice I received. I thought. How? If I knew how, I would. I longed for help.

There wasn't anyone I could confide in. I believed if I could just speak with God, He would hear and help me, but I didn't know how to call on Him. I tried to pray but my prayers seemed to bounce off the ceiling and stay with me.

---

1   2 Timothy 1:7

Chapter 2

Many Paths

In spite of my health issues, I had a great husband, two well-behaved children and everything I needed. One would possibly think my life was completely happy if they measured it by what they could see. If there was something I wanted, we managed to get it. No, we didn't have much money. We had good credit, but misuse of credit was paving a path to a dead end street.

I always felt weak and defeated. After spending time with my mother, seeing her awesome talent, I wanted to be artistic like her. Sometimes when I felt the urge to be creative, I would begin a project which appealed to me and for awhile it progressed well, but gradually, it seemed as though I was overshadowed by a dark cloud. Little by little, I would lose my enthusiasm. I felt like I was spiraling downward, until I put my work aside. My projects were always unfinished. Then depression and defeat came dragging me further downward, like quicksand.

In retrospect, I realize I was blind. I guess that is what the Bible means when it says that we cannot see the gospel of Jesus because our minds are blinded by the enemy.[2]

When we had been married about three years, Eddie was two and Robin was a tiny newborn weighing just five pounds, we had a modest

---

2 2 Corinthians 4:3–4

house built for us in a pleasant neighborhood in Savannah, Georgia. We filled it with new furniture. It wasn't the most expensive furniture, but we strapped ourselves so tight money wise, food was in short supply.

We had pleasant neighbors and were comfortable except when it rained. Then it flooded up to our driveway. There were poisonous snakes and even an alligator swimming around in the water. Permission to build our subdivision should never have been given. The neighbors were protesting to the city officials. Our nest was being shaken, and we were ready to move.

We sold our house, making just enough money to pay off our bills and rented a large white, cinder block house in the country. It was one of five homes, each on an acre of land. The houses were attractive and it was quiet. I loved living in the country.

I went out to my clothesline one day which was in the middle of my large backyard, and as I began hanging the clothes, I glanced to my left and saw about ten or twelve large, full grown turkeys running toward me. Their eyes were wide and wild looking. I thought, they look hungry, and I'm their dinner!

I picked up my basket and sprinted for safety. I ran inside slamming my screen door as they stood on my porch looking inside, gobbling at me.

My heart was beating so fast; I had to sit down to catch my breath. So much for living in the peaceful country!

I asked one of the neighbors about the turkeys and was told, she always took a treat for them when she went out to hang her clothes. Therefore, I was right; they were hungry and expecting to eat when they saw me. I never fed them and was very cautious when I had to hang my clothes. These turkeys mysteriously disappeared in November just before Thanksgiving. Wonder where they went?

It was winter 1959, when the weather turned cold, and the cinderblock walls became damp. There was only one small heater located in the large living room. The heat didn't circulate to the other parts of the house. Even keeping the children dressed warm, they became ill. To my dismay, we began shopping once again for another house to rent which we could keep warmer.

We found an old house in Thunderbolt located on the east side of Savannah. It was known for its shrimp boat traffic. You could watch the shrimp boats as they moved up and down the river paralleling the main street. Our home was less than a block off the river. We were now nearer Savannah and my family, which made my mother happy.

Even though our house was warm and comfortable, the children were still sick, especially Eddie, who was now 3 years old. He was taking medicine and under the care of our doctor. The doctor believed he had the flu. He grew worse, running a high temperature and finally became so ill, when he opened his eyes, they were glazed. He wasn't aware of anything around him including me and was given medicine, so he could retain a little water to prevent dehydration. I could only get him to swallow one Tablespoon of water at a time. That night Stuart told me they would put him in the hospital because he wasn't improving, and they couldn't give him any more of the medicine.

Again, I became fearful. Robin was still ill but not as bad as Eddie. We had Eddie sleeping between us, so we could give him constant care. Stuart went into check on Robin, I began to pray. I didn't know until several years later that Stuart also was praying at the same time in the other room. In my prayer, I told the Lord if He would make my son well, I would give Eddie to Him to do His work. I didn't even know at that time, what God's work was.

When Stuart and I were trying to go back to sleep, Eddie opened his eyes and said, "Mama, will you fix me a *hangerbur* for breakfast?" I put my hand on his forehead, and it was dry and cool. God had healed him!

I was shocked! I was standing in the stark, obvious reality that there is a God, and He hears and answers prayer! I didn't know anything about God healing people. This was the first recognizable time I can pinpoint God dealing with us, drawing us to Him.

In May, 1960, we were transferred to Dover Air Force Base in Delaware. Robin would be one year old this month and in two months, Eddie would be four. We found Dover to be a beautiful, quaint little town. Mennonites rode their horse drawn carriages through the streets. They kept their land clean and neat, and sold their goods at the farmer's market. It was so peaceful. I knew that if peace could be found, I would find it in Dover. Later I saw an interview with a man in the Virgin Islands. He said, "Many people come to the Islands searching for peace and are disappointed. Before one can find peace, they must have it in their heart. You don't get peace from your surroundings. You take your discontent with you wherever you go. Find peace and then come here." I found this to be true.

We heard beforehand, housing was scarce. Many were living in old, remodeled farm houses, so we decided, since our children had been so sick just three months before, we would buy a mobile home. We traded our furniture as a down payment on the trailer and had it transported to Dover. It couldn't have been easier for us. We stayed in a motel until it arrived, then we walked into our familiar home with everything in place.

Meanwhile, I started a letter to my mother letting her know we had arrived safely. When we got in bed that night, we were tired and in deep sleep when, for some unknown reason, Stuart, Eddie and I, sat up at the same time in bed. The trailer and everything in it, was shaking. When it subsided, we laid back down, still asleep, all together, again, at the same time.

The next morning, Stuart reported to the base, I was working inside the house and Eddie was playing in the yard. I thought I heard something vaguely familiar, and then suddenly I remembered what happened while we were asleep the night before. The trailer began to shake; the brass plates on the wall began to wobble. I ran to the door to get Eddie. I wasn't used to the doors, I frantically struggled, but I couldn't get it open. I peered out the window and saw Eddie running for all he was worth finally diving head first under the trailer. We were parked near the end of the base's runway! It had been nighttime when we arrived. When the airplanes flew over, it seemed like they were just above our electric power poles.

At a later date, Joann and Earl were stationed in New Jersey and they came for a visit. I forgot to warn them about the planes. They were sleeping on the sofa when, the brass plates on the wall started vibrating, and then the trailer began to shake. Joann reached over to grab Earl, but instead found her hand full of short, coarse hair. Then, Joann, Earl and Peppi sat up wondering, what is happening? Our full grown German shepherd had crawled up between them on the small couch.

Our trailer park neighbors, who were military, told us we had a southern trailer, and it couldn't take the winters in Delaware. This disturbed us due to our children's poor health the previous winter. The white, fluffy snow began to fall, and they assured us it would only be on the ground a short time, so enjoy it. Being from the south, rarely had I seen snow. Stuart was originally from Chicago so this wasn't new to him. We did enjoy the snow, but we also worried about the winter months ahead. To everyone's surprise and our delight, our warm, tight southern trailer chugged right along. It wasn't long before we were pulling in the northern trailers water lines to warm them up. They had frozen. We were cozy and warm.

In this peaceful quiet town, I was more miserable than ever. The airmen were being sent overseas for what was to be short times, so they didn't take luggage, and they didn't return for months. My nerves were getting worse but I didn't tell Stuart. For a brief time, I lost vision in my right eye. I was apprehensive about Stuart being sent overseas for duty. I decided to sell Avon Products in order to help with our finances. Going out into the surrounding area I met new people, mostly military. Hearing the many complaints of military wives, I grew more anxious. We decided this wasn't the life for us, so when the time came for re-enlistment; we decided we would get out of the military for good. This was a serious decision because it was Stuart's career. We hadn't made other career plans; we just took a step of faith, which was scary because without God, we didn't even have a faith! We were just living life the best we could. I felt even more insecure and fearful.

We were now civilians eager to settle down to an independent life. We moved back to Thunderbolt, but this time we would be living in our southern trailer. We settled in a park even closer to the river. Next door to us was a military family. They had a little boy the same age as Eddie. One day I heard he was seriously ill with asthma. I went over for a cup of coffee with his mother. As we were sitting at the kitchen talking, a very strange thing happened: words started coming down into the top of my head like a ticker tape. I wondered about this but just kept saying the words that came to me. I told her about Eddie's illness and how the Lord had healed him. When the words finished, I broke into tears because I hadn't told anyone about this before. Stuart and I hadn't even discussed it between ourselves. I had forgotten about the healing until I had this strange experience. It was as if that experience had been blanked out of my mind completely

It was at that time I decided we needed God's help. I listened, waiting to hear where He might be found. I knew there were many religions, and they couldn't all be right. Without doubt I believed in the God of the *Bible* and Jesus Christ, his Son. This kept me in the confines of the Christian religion, but which denomination?

I had weakly suggested, at times, we should go to church. My husband wasn't agreeable. And although he wouldn't stop me from going, I wouldn't go without him. He needed it more than I since; after all, I was the one to make the suggestion. Furthermore, I wouldn't have anyone to hide behind if I went alone so, we stayed home.

On television one evening, the news reported a group of people waiting on top of a mountain. The watchers were telling the reporters the Lord told them He was coming on this particular date to take them home to be with Him.

Being ignorant of the truth of the *Bible*, I was getting in and out of bed to look at the sky throughout the night. What if Jesus does come tonight, and I'm not ready to meet him? I was afraid I was going to die and would be in the presence of the Holy God in my sinful condition. Thank God He didn't come that night because I was right. I wasn't ready to meet Jesus.

Before we left the military, I made a *To Do List* of the things we would do when we returned to Savannah. I don't remember everything on my list, it was only one page. But I do remember the last thing was *join a church*.

I believed in the God of the *Bible*, even though I didn't know the *Bible*. I knew it was the Holy Book, and I believed Jesus died on the cross. After all, I lived in a country where all of these facts were displayed in our schools and communities at their proper times of the year. I always went to church at Christmas and Easter when I was young, never questioning whether Jesus arose from the dead. I didn't analyze that fact. I just believed it. But, I also believed George Washington never told a lie! I didn't lie, mother would have killed me. I accepted the fact George Washington never told a lie or at least, he never got caught. Maybe he had a tough mother, too!

I wanted to talk to the God I had heard about in Sunday school from the *Bible* stories. As a child I went to church when I wanted to, but my family did not go to church. Once when I was thirteen, I surrendered my life to Jesus Christ. I didn't understand what I had done, but I knew what I felt when I went to the altar at the Baptist church. No one talked with me, but I later learned someone had contacted my mother and she told them I was too young to understand the commitment I would be making. Because of her decision, I thought I couldn't belong to the church so I couldn't belong to Jesus, and that ended that. But, it didn't end that. I didn't understand something eternal had taken place in my soul when I responded to the altar call. It wasn't the preacher, but God's Holy Spirit wooing me to himself.

I watched people who did go to church. I just couldn't relate them to being like people in the stories from the *Bible*. I guess in my heart, I discounted them and kept watching and listening for someone who admired God and lived like those in the *Bible*.

When I went to a church, and they sang like they meant what they were singing, I loved it. This didn't happen very often. If the preacher preached like he meant what he was saying, I loved it. This didn't happen very often either.

I guess what I am trying to say is, I was a good girl because mainly my mother was a good mom when it came to teaching and insisting that I be good. I didn't even dare to think improperly. She was also consistent. She wasn't one way one day and another way the next. I knew what she expected and performed. However, in spite of that, I sinned. The Bible tells us that everyone sins. [3]

There's a story in the *Bible* about a young man who came to Jesus and asked, "What must I do to be saved?" Jesus gave him a list. He was a good boy, and he told Jesus that he had done all these things from his youth. He looked at him, saw his heart, and loved him. But, the boy knew something major was missing in his life. He didn't know what, but he knew he didn't have it. Jesus nailed it down for him. "When Jesus heard this, he said to him, 'You still lack one thing. Sell everything you have and give to the poor, and you will have treasure in Heaven. Then come, follow me.'" The young man turned and went away sad. Love of material things would cost him his soul. [4]

Now, here we were, out of the Air Force and back in Savannah, but my list wasn't working for us. As we tried to live our life, nothing

---

3   Romans 3:23
4   Mark 10:18-25

seemed to go right. Jobs were not available so Stuart decided to become a trucker. We borrowed money and invested in getting the truck ready to ride. It was a medium green color, shiny without any flaws and we were so proud of it. On the one and only trip, Stuart returned home, walking in a stooped over position. All he said as he entered the door was, "Don't say anything!" Believe me…I said not one word, but my heart sank to the floor.

Chapter 3

Seek and You Shall Find

The payments on the truck were crushing. I was so discouraged by this time, as Stuart lay in bed sick with a virus; I went and got my list. I put *Go to church* to the top of the *To Do's*. We were a sinking ship and only God could help. After all our efforts to get on our feet failed, Stuart, and I was in agreement about going to church. We needed help beyond our own abilities.

We chose the Baptist church nearest our apartment, a small, wooden structure on a side street. I had never seen it before. It was far from fancy. I didn't care. My only reason to be there was to let God know I meant business. I was willing to do whatever it took to serve him. I felt my life wouldn't work right otherwise.

We went for two consecutive Sundays. The first Sunday, the children were miserable and the only way I could stay at church, was to be in the nursery with them. I was in the sanctuary during service with Stuart the second Sunday. We sat on the back pew. Even though the room was small, the acoustics were poor, so I couldn't hear what was being preached. I was bored, but still determined to find God. He knew where I was, how I felt and why I was there.

The day before the third Sunday, word reached Stuart, someone wanted to see our now-idle truck. If it was what they wanted, they would buy it. Deep in my heart I believed God was moving in our lives because we were finally willing to obey him. However, the man was only available on Sunday morning. Oh, Shucks! I'd have to miss church! Church bored me and I got restless during the service, but I had determined to find God for my life regardless of what I had to go through. I wanted to speak with God and didn't know how to make contact. I was desperate.

Early Sunday morning, my husband left for his appointment. I knew God was selling our truck, but I had no idea what was going to happen to me while that transaction was taking place.

The children were playing in their bedrooms with their toys. I was a little restless with nothing to do now that our plans for the day were changed. I went into the living room, picked up a deck of cards and began a game of solitaire. This I could play without concentrating.

As I sat there shuffling the cards, I heard church chimes playing. I have always loved church chimes. Where are they coming from? I didn't know there was a church near here. Strange, I hadn't heard them before.

All of a sudden, an awesome peace filled the room; I was hardly breathing, and sat completely still. This indescribable peace seemed out of this world, and it truly was. I was afraid to move. It might stop.

Then the Lord's voice spoke, "*Get up, get dressed, and go to church!*" I felt so good, I did just that. I even cooked a hot breakfast for the children, even though I knew if I heard real church chimes, it was already late.

As the children and I were walking toward the car I thought, I don't drive anymore! I ignored that fact and proceeded to drive toward the little church we had been attending. When we reached the main drive, I started to make a left hand turn when the Lord's voice spoke again.

He said, "*No, turn right!*"

I knew which church he wanted me to attend. Out of all the churches nearby, I just knew which one the Lord meant. I didn't need words to tell me. It was *knowledge*, which is one of the gifts of the Holy Spirit. [5]

When we entered the church building, my children co-operated, and went quietly into separate nurseries. Amazing, but everything happening was amazing.

---

5   1 Corinthians 5:17

I entered the sanctuary of the large Baptist church. Everyone was well dressed, the ladies even wore hats. I sat on the back pew, and when they began to sing, I felt the good feeling I felt as a child in church. They sang like they meant it. The minister began to preach, and he preached like he meant every word he said. Again I was pleased, that is…until he got to the end of the sermon. Now I didn't feel the peace anymore. I felt like someone who had been lured out on the end of a limb just before the sawing began. I was agitated, and felt like running out of the building.

The congregation started to sing while the minister gave the altar call. I recognized the hymn and it touched my heart. "Come home, come home, ye who are weary, come home. Softly, and tenderly Jesus is calling, calling 'Oh sinner, come home."

From my left the Lord's voice spoke, insisting: "*Go now! Go Now!*"

I pondered this momentarily, and then another voice spoke from my right side, saying, "No, not now–later!"

I was perplexed. Now there were two voices. What should I do? I sat through altar calls before and felt a pull to go down, but I'd never had a voice speak to me, and now there were two!

"Come home, come home–," the people sang,

I thought, I'm not holy and I don't want to be like a nun. I'm not a hypocrite.

"Softly and tenderly, Jesus–," the congregation continued singing.[6]

If I go down to the altar in front of all these people, I'll be making a commitment I can't keep. I might be holy till Tuesday, but I know before Friday I'll fail.

Then the Lord's voice from my left spoke again: "*If you don't go now, you'll be put in a mental institution!*"

This was not a threat, but a fact. No one but God knew how bad my nerves were. I experienced flashbacks of my life. At a very depressed time of my life, impulsively, yet coldly deliberate, I sinned thinking it would solve my problem. At that moment, I wasn't thinking about God, or right and wrong, only of solving my several years of torment. I didn't realize how the serious results of this wrong choice would affect my mental health.

---

6 Hymn, Softly and Tenderly by Will L. Thompson, 1847–1909

When my thoughts returned to the present, I am only twenty-five years old, and I've already made a mess of my life. My helplessness was too much for me to cope with and I had come to an end.

Then in my heart and mind, I spoke to God, "Lord, if you can take my life and put it back together, you can have it!" He knew I regretted sinning, and that I was truly sorry.

I stood, glancing to my right was a lady with a beautiful, gentle smile filled with compassion, and I slipped sideways out of the pew to go down to the minister. The singing had been prolonged because Dr. Meadows felt someone was going to come forward.

As I moved, unexpectedly, I felt ropes break off of my chest. I was jerked when they pulled off. Until that moment, I hadn't realized I was bound with strong ropes. Suddenly, I was free and began to cry and oh, did I shake! As I reached the pastor, I held on his arm to remain steady on my feet. "I was free indeed!" The *Bible* tells us "So if the Son sets you free, you will be free indeed." I was free, even before leaving the pew, before reaching the minister, before joining the church, before anything because I did what He told me to do. [7]

Several years later, I found the scripture: "His own iniquities shall take the wicked himself, and he shall be holden with the cords of his sins." Sins are not small things. They are ropes which tie a person up. They constrict, disable and cause them to be helpless. Furthermore, they'll steal the mind. [8]

Everyone came and shook my hand to welcome me as I was voted into the church as a member. I thought as they shook my hand, if they only knew what had just happened to me, they would be having a party! What I also didn't know: the *Bible* says, *Heaven was rejoicing over my coming home! Heaven was having a party because of me!* I felt it in my soul! I was free! I was in right standing with God at last!

I left the church building a new person. No more bad nerves, no more anger against people, and no more gossip. "Therefore if any man be in Christ, he is a new creature: old things are passed away; behold, all things are become new." I was so elated; I struggled to keep myself balanced as I walked. I was truly a new creation. [9]

---

7 John 8:36

8 Proverbs 5:22

9 2 Corinthians 5:17

I put my children in the car, and as I was driving home, it was as though I was encased in strong, impenetrable armor, made of a warm cloud, soft to my body. As I pondered what had happened, I realized my sins had been forgiven and God had heard and answered my plea.

Then the Lord's voice spoke, "*I will never let anything hurt you again.*"

Chapter 4

Where You Lead,

I Will Follow

I was amazed at the reality of God; His words were expected, but not his personal touch. I was surprised. He'd been near me all the time, and loved me in spite of what he knew about me. My encounter with him was dynamic. I had harbored deep anger and resentment toward some people, yet his loving presence was so overwhelming. There wasn't any criticism or condemnation from him, just total acceptance. All of my bitterness was washed away and replaced by deep satisfaction and contentment. Then, as now, I wanted never to do anything to disappoint him, nor disrupt our relationship.

When I arrived home from church, I noticed my neighbor in her yard. Hannah was young when she married her sweetheart. He was an Airman without much rank so their income was meager. They supplemented their living by managing our apartments. She had told me about her poor health. They had three small children, and as young as she was, she'd already experienced a nervous breakdown.

"Eddie, take Robin in the house while I go over to Hannah's a minute, and then I'll come and fix lunch."

"Hi, how are you?"

"Good." Eyeing my dress, she asked, "Where've you been so early?"

"To church. We don't usually go, but something unusual happened this morning."

"Oh?"

"Yes, and I want to tell you about it." I told her everything as it happened.

"Really? I believe James would like to hear about this. Tomorrow night, when he comes home, after supper, if I call, do you suppose you could come over?"

"Yes. Just call. I better hurry and start lunch, Stu will be home soon."

"Sure," she answered looking around for her children. She had been listening so attentively to what I was saying, we had lost track of time.

I hurried home to see what my kids were doing. As I went, I noticed I was trembling. My mind was racing wondering what Hannah was thinking. She appeared to be interested, but I know what I thought when I was a teen-ager and a married lady in our neighborhood made a brief comment about Jesus. She was a favorite person among the teens. I believed she probably had a mental problem and needed religion to help her through her crisis. I was sad for her, but on the other hand, I was flippant. It was good she couldn't read my mind. Now I began to wonder if Hannah might be thinking the same about me.

Stuart would be home soon, and I was worried. I never made major decisions alone. I had not only gone to church without him, but they accepted me as a new member after the altar call! How was I going to tell him?

I could see when he came through the door, he was happy and I knew the truck was sold. I felt such relief and was free to share about our going to church and joining, but I didn't tell him everything I'd experienced.

He was still excited and said, "Great, we'll all go to church and be a Christian family!"

I was startled and when I opened my mouth to protest and explain in detail what happened to me, I felt to say nothing. He couldn't just join the church to be a Christian, but I held my peace.

We attended church that night as a family and sat near the front. Before preaching his sermon, Dr. Meadows said, "Mr. Osland, we got your wife this morning. We'll get you next." Everyone laughed including us. We were warmed by their acceptance and felt an oneness with them.

I began to think about our friends. If they had experienced anything like this with God, they would have told us. I felt I must tell them how real God is, and that he's not far off or indifferent. He sees and knows everything, and cares about us.

I wrote each one a letter and shared about my Sunday morning. I called some, along with a few of my relatives, on the telephone. I knew they would be surprised. Remembering my thoughts about my neighbor, I felt I was taking a risk of losing their friendships, but on the other hand, what kind of friend would I be if I didn't tell them, so they could have the same wonderful love for themselves. It was worth the risk. I loved and had confidence in my friends.

My friends had different reactions. One said we were accepting what the church was telling us and everything they said wasn't necessarily so. They were trying to reason with us from their point of view, but it didn't seem to affect our friendship.

Our correspondence remained intact except for one couple, Brenda and Marshall who I corresponded with in the future. We had visited them before my spiritual birth. Marshall had gone through brain surgery, and was still recovering. They were a young couple and their church had finished building their new house for them, since he wasn't physically able. Not only was I impressed by the love shown by their church, but when they spoke of God's personal love and care, coupled with seeing Marshall's obvious disability, I was overwhelmed. Soon we left to go to my mothers, and when we entered her front door, I hardly made it to the bathroom before bursting into tears and sobs. Marshall's life was in peril, and yet they spoke so lovingly about God. I realized I had so much to be thankful for, and the contrast of our lives was great. Their witness impacted my life with power paving the way for the day of my glorious experience. We never had the opportunity to see them again.

The next evening, Hannah called asking me to come over for a few minutes. When I walked in the door, James was standing in the middle of the room with a smug look on his face. Hannah put the coffee on while he and I made small talk. As we drank our coffee, Hannah said she had told James a little about what happened to me, and he wanted to hear more.

I began sharing and started to tremble. It was a little distracting, but my mind was sharp and clear as I told my story. James still wasn't acting like himself. I couldn't figure why until he began asking me the meaning behind a scripture out of the *Bible*.

This surprised me somewhat because I wasn't familiar with the *Bible*, so I couldn't give him an answer. I could only tell him what I had experienced on Sunday morning. When I was apologetic explaining my ignorance, he began acting more like himself.

"I was raised in church. My whole family goes. I just don't go." he said.

Our evening ended shortly after he said this. As I went home, I felt sad. I didn't know if he even heard what I had said. That night after everyone had gone to bed; I went and stood by my window looking out at the sky. Weeping, I told the Lord, I felt like I had failed him and my neighbor by my ignorance. I asked him to open the scriptures to me so this wouldn't happen again.

Our life took on a routine which included going to church every time the doors were open. We relished our new life. It had only one big flaw: There hadn't been a spiritual change in my husband. Stuart was a nice guy and fit in so well. He began taking a prominent role in our Sunday school discussions and didn't seem to realize he was lacking something major in his life. Everyone liked him and he was comfortable, but I wasn't happy because, I knew he needed to experience God, and I was anxious for him. I pondered what I could do to encourage him in this direction. I found a tract (a small pamphlet) about Hell. I left it on the back of the toilet where I knew sooner or later he would notice and read it. To my dismay nothing was ever said!

Our pastor was so powerful in his preaching. I especially remember one Sunday evening before the altar call he said, "How many of you know for certain, you will get home tonight?"

Tension began to mount within me, is God going to let us get killed in an automobile accident because Stuart won't surrender? I became more anxious for him, but I didn't say anything, I just prayed.

One day, we were arguing, and as I went into the bedroom I heard a loud noise. I went into the kitchen to find what it was. I saw this hole in the newly painted wall.

"What happened?" I asked.

"Nothing. I just tripped and my elbow went through the wall."

I knew better. He was angry with me and had put his fist through the wall. I was so disappointed. Later, he told someone this episode showed him he didn't yet have Christ in his life. Stuart's own words were, "I had seen a change in Tommie's life, but there hadn't been a change in mine." This led up to his encounter with Jesus Christ.

Six months had passed since my spiritual birthday when I was born again, and tonight we were in a Sunday night service. The pastor was closing, and I was praying, when the Holy Spirit's presence, his warmth, surrounded me. I began to shake and had to sit down. I knew my husband was going to respond to the altar call. A teen-age girl sitting on my left began nudging me with her elbow whispering excitedly, "Did you know Stuart went down?" But, I felt God's presence so powerfully, I was afraid to talk or even open my eyes. This was a "holy moment with God." When I did open my eyes, Stuart was up front shaking hands with the minister. I had a new husband driving me home that night. At last, we were the Christian family Stuart wanted.

Stuart began reading his *Bible*. As of yet, I had not. Judy, our neighbor and friend, began visiting on a regular basis. I thought perhaps the Holy Spirit was drawing her so she could hear our story. We shared with her about finding Jesus as our Lord. Stuart and I hadn't yet shared all our personal details with each other.

Judy had two sons and a young daughter, a toddler. She and Stuart would read and discuss the *Bible* together. I have to admit, at these times, I irritably thought, is this going to be our life from now on. Will everything we do center on reading and discussing the *Bible?* I felt left out because I hadn't yet begun to read for myself. I guess I feared it still would be difficult to understand as it had been for me before giving my life to Jesus.

One Sunday morning, Judy decided to go to church with us. During the morning service, Judy and her youngest son gave their lives to Jesus. We were so happy and then that same evening, the eldest son did likewise.

We were still having a difficult time with our finances, I had supposed now that our lives were in order with God, it would be easier. Well, to my surprise, we were still struggling. Stuart had exhausted his field for work, so once again we were in position to change locations. We were puzzled, but accepted this as God's plan for our life.

Stuart said his mother would help if we went to Chicago. He didn't want to live there, but we could save until we were financially able to move to Minnesota. He had family living there also who would help us settle. We agreed to pray about these places and ask God what we should do.

I tried to contact Stuart's mother several times and there was no answer. I was concerned because she was elderly, had a business in her home and should have been there. I knew our coming to Chicago would please her.

There was a visiting minister speaking at church. He said he had a sermon prepared, but felt led by the Holy Spirit rather to share an experience he'd had. He said he was to catch a train. When he got to the station, there were three trains: one was going to Chicago, Illinois; another was going to St. Paul, Minnesota. The third train was going to Los Angeles, California. When he finished his story saying the train to Los Angeles was the train he was to catch, we knew this couldn't be for us.

Then we received a letter from Stuart's sister, Avis, who lived in Los Angeles. We didn't usually communicate. No one knew of our struggle, not even my parents who lived nearby. Avis had enclosed some check stubs from her job and told us there was plenty of work out there, and we could stay with her until we got settled. At that moment we knew this was God once again directing our path.

I don't know where Stuart's mother was when I tried to reach her, but I was thankful she wasn't at home. It would have been a great disappointment for our plans to have changed.

When the realization that we were actually moving to Los Angeles, impacted me, I had mixed emotions. My mother's sister, Billie, had married, a soldier we hardly knew when she was only eighteen years old. She moved to Reno, Nevada, and I felt like she had been swallowed alive. A member of our family had disappeared. I never saw and rarely heard of her again. It was as if she never existed except in a fleeting memory.

My mother didn't take the news of our going to California kindly. She strongly opposed our move, and made it very difficult for me. Whenever I called her on the phone, you could feel the coldness in her voice. I've always tried to please my mom, but now I had surrendered my life to Jesus and would be obedient to Him above everyone. I had to lift my eyes higher than anything or anyone in this world. Stuart, bless his heart, even took the *Bible* and went over to try and explain to her that this move was being directed by the Lord. He used Abraham's experience of leaving his people, traveling not even knowing where he was to go. This didn't impress my mother. [10] [11]

A Christian brother who knew of our pending move and opposition told us that it was the enemy of our souls trying to hinder us from obeying God. I had never heard of spiritual warfare before. To think of my mother being manipulated by the Devil was terrible, but realizing that she was being used to prevent us from leaving, I could remove her personally from the situation, this made it endurable.

---

10 Genesis 12:1
11 Hebrews 11:8

Chapter 5

New Beginnings

We knew the directions we had received, with confirmations, were from the Lord, and we must continue to follow his leading. We had surrendered our lives totally to his desire and nothing must hinder our obedience.

We planned to leave in August. We didn't have an air conditioner or a spare tire, and we also were having trouble with our car. It was almost a daily experience to reattach the starter, and there was a leak in the radiator.

Due to lack of funds, we planned to stop at grocery stores for sandwich makings and something to drink rather than eat at restaurants. We also planned to sleep in our station wagon. We knew it was going to be a hot, difficult trip.

I worked in the medical records department at a hospital. One day Dr. Miller and Dr. Sanders were in the office. "This is a hot time of the year to go across the desert," Dr. Sanders said as he was searching for his surgery notes.

Dr. Miller asked me when we were leaving.

Before I could answer, Dr. Sanders said, "They're leaving in August! When we went, my kid's lips cracked and bled. It was so dry and hot! It's going to be tough, Kiddo!"

"Yeah," Dr. Miller agreed.

My mind began to race. Maybe we should wait for cooler weather. I wished they hadn't said anything. I had never been in the desert. Once again, my imagination began to roam, I struggled to remember, I trusted the Lord, and he would take care of us. I wasn't looking forward to this trip, but we couldn't continue living without a better job. My job did little more than pay for childcare. We definitely believed the mother should be in the home with the children.

We set a date and began to give away and sell our few belongings. Surprisingly, we began receiving money by mail and other sources. The Lord supplied what money was needed, and we would be able to stay in motels and eat in restaurants. This helped me relax knowing we would be comfortable during the night hours.

The night before we left, we met Jay, Lucy, and their young son, Ronnie. They were a fellow church member's family, who lived in Los Angeles. They and their son were new Christians who loved Jesus. Little did we know what inspirational and loving friends they would be to us? We were to spend many all night get-togethers in the Bible and what a solid foundation was laid for our lives. What fellowship! What love!

We packed as much as we could in and on our car. We said we looked like the Beverly Hillbillies, and we probably did. These were necessities for setting up our home in California.

To compensate for the lack of air conditioning, we put a metal humidifier full of water in the window by the front passenger seat. As the car moved, air went over the water cooling the air. The main problem with this was: when we turned a corner, the water splashed over the passenger, which was me! Yes, it especially cooled me!

We made it across town, then out a short distance on the highway, when Stuart stopped the car, and got out to check the tires. They were mashed down and hot to his touch. He came to the window and said, "We have to unload, or we won't make it with the tires like this, and we don't have a spare."

Since our belongings were all packed in boxes like baby pictures, baby shoes, handmade spinning wheel Stuart's grandfather had made, unimportant things like that, "Boo hoo!" You know what I'm saying, mothers, don't you?" We didn't have the time to go through the boxes. We had to unload quickly.

There were several shacks up the embankment off the side of the highway. As we unpacked the car, we saw curious brown faces, young and old, peering over the grassy edge, watching to see what we were doing. Stuart motioned for them to come down, and we gave them our treasures. I would have kept the pictures and shoes, had I thought about them, but we were in such a hurry. There are circumstances where you have to place things on God's altar.

As we drove away from these families, we sensed great relief. The extreme urgency to leave quickly had lifted. We sensed complete serenity and peace. Our daughter, Robin, who was three, was sitting on top of our big, white family *Bible* between us in the front seat. Eddie, who was five, was quietly sitting in the back, looking out the window. Silently, we drove onward, our car filled with serenity.

Stuart spoke softly, breaking the silence, "Honey?"

"Yes?"

"I feel God's hands over mine, and if I take my hands off the steering wheel, he will drive it, himself."

I didn't answer because God's presence was so strong. It wasn't until we had given everything away that the Holy Spirit filled our car. This more than reassured us, we were in God's perfect will.

From that time to four and a half days later, we experienced God's mercy and divine protection. As we drove west on Highway 80, a wreck could have occurred when the left front tire on a car coming toward us blew out. By all logic, it should have pulled the car into our lane causing a head-on collision. Instead, it neither swerved nor pulled, but settled slowly to the side of the road. Stuart marveled at this.

I was in awe when we entered New Mexico. I had never seen such magnificent sights. They took my breath away. There wasn't another car in sight as we drove through the towering canyons. It seemed like there wasn't anyone in the world except for us in our little car. I felt small like an ant looking up at the tall overpowering mountains. Who could ever doubt there is a God?

As we were well into the trip, we stopped to refresh ourselves; people were saying how the rain had cooled the temperature. Even when we got to Needles, California, in the desert, the hottest point of our trip, everyone was remarking how it never rained this time of the year. We were reminded of the Hebrews in their exodus from Egypt and the cloud going before them. It rained the day before we arrived, cooling the desert before us. He was moving mighty in our behalf.

As we came out of the San Bernardino Mountains, I pointed and said, "Look at those brown clouds. My eyes are burning!"

"Those are not clouds," Stuart said, "its smog!"

I hadn't seen smog before, and as we merged onto the freeway, I had never seen traffic like that either. Cars were traveling at high speeds and very close to each other, moving in and out of the lanes. It frightened me; I was holding on to the seat and wouldn't move. I felt like I was on a wild ride in an amusement park.

"I have to go to the potty!" Eddie whined.

"Just wait a minute." I answered, knowing the potty was in back of the seats in the station wagon. They both complained until finally, I forced myself to loosen my grip on the seat, so I could move and see to their potty needs. Poor babies!

We drove and drove. The cars were like an endless river. Stuart said, "I'm getting off here to ask for directions."

We pulled into a nearby filling station. My husband called to the attendant. "Could you tell me where I can find Crenshaw Boulevard?"

The man just glared at him like he was crazy and pointed up to the street sign.

"Crenshaw Boulevard!" Avis lived on Crenshaw, just a few blocks away.

Only God could have caused Stuart to spontaneously pull off of the freeway on the right boulevard just a couple of blocks from his sister's house.

We pulled up the drive into the back parking area behind her house. We went in and enjoyed a short visit before she told Stuart to go and move the car. These parking places were assigned to other tenants. When he went to move the car, the starter was laying on the pavement under the car. We hadn't experienced the first bit of trouble on the entire trip of four and a half days and 2600 miles! I know a miracle when I see one and this was it! However, that's just natural for our great God! It's a miracle to us!

All the way to Los Angeles our children droned over and over, "Are we there yet?" It was a long trip and at last we said, "We are there!" What a relief!

Chapter 6

A Strange Land

There I was a southern belle in Los Angeles, California. What a shock! It was like a foreign country, and I had never lived on a boulevard before. The traffic was constant, day and night. I wondered if they ever slept.

Avis, and Kim, her daughter, and Eddie, her son, were very hospitable, and received us with open arms. Kim and Eddie were teenagers and fun to be with. They were preparing to leave on a train for a short vacation to Chicago to visit relatives. The timing seemed to be inappropriate, yet it would give us some time to relax and acclimatize ourselves to the area.

When they returned, we began our schedule for living together. Since everyone either worked or went to school, I began cooking and doing some of the housework. I was comfortable with this role.

Avis' house had been remodeled into a duplex, and a neighbor, who was like a member of the family, lived in the other half. He was a unique fellow, a real Hollywood character. By that I mean his jobs were spontaneous. He was in and out of entertainment situations, parties and even did investigative work. It was quite exciting listening to his adventurous stories, but sometimes I wondered if they were altogether accurate. His name was Ed, but since we had so many with that name in our family, we called him Big Ed. He played a major role in endearing our niece to the entertainment community. He was a father figure to her and her brother. He was an easy person to love.

Early one morning after everyone had left for work, I was in the kitchen peeling potatoes for dinner. Big Ed, his slouch hat pulled down almost covering his eyes trying to block out the bright light, shirt recklessly hanging out his long, baggy Bermuda shorts came down the hallway with his flip flops clapping against the floor announcing his presence. He came into the kitchen and stood beside me at the sink.

Staring in disbelief he asked, "What is that?"

"A potato," I answered.

"A real potato?"

I looked at him and laughed. "What other kind is there?"

"I haven't seen a real potato in years. I've only seen them from a box. I can't believe it!" He exclaimed as he walked out of the kitchen shaking his head.

Bewildered, I watched him leave. His statement made me think; maybe I was out of step with the times, I knew I was out of my comfort zone here in Los Angeles. I was beginning to feel like the Hillbilly, Harry, Stuart's brother-in-law, had called us. Some of the excitement of this new adventure was beginning to wear thin.

I'm very sensitive to people and their disgruntlements, and in the early mornings, people weren't ready to put on smiling faces, especially before a cup of coffee. We were seven people living in a space meant for just three. It's always difficult living with others. Stuart was working alongside Harry who seemed to take pleasure in using lots of profanity. We didn't know Avis had told her friends, that her brother and family were real religious and to watch their language. This seemed to inspire Harry even more.

We shared what the Lord had done in our lives when the doors were open, but tried not to preach. Nevertheless, the quarters were getting noticeably tight. I felt completely out of my element.

It was 1962, and I discovered a freedom I enjoyed in Los Angeles. While on my way to the super market one morning, I encountered a black man painting a building. We must have made eye contact because he stopped working to speak with me. We had a nice conversation, and then I went on my way. I marveled at the freedom I experienced because I was born and reared in Savannah, Georgia, in 1936. It was before integration and my parents and grandparents taught me their way of life which greatly restricted my interactions with people of color.

As I write this, I'm aware of wanting to explain so that you, especially my young readers, would understand what it was like for me to live in the south during the time of segregation. My desire is to protect those I love from criticism and for the reader to understand how they received instructions from their parents and culture which they in turn, attempted to pass on to me. It was a way of life.

I was generally obedient, but some things happened spontaneously, and I received their correction. I was trained to a way I eventually couldn't accept, and was very aware when I disobeyed the rules set down by my well-meaning loved ones. No one had to correct me; it was an inner awareness, a conviction.

Therefore, by reason of my upbringing, I couldn't have this experience of conversing in public with a black man without feeling I was being observed and having fear of my family finding out. I liked this freedom and felt it was good.

God is a wonderful artist, and loves all colors. He has created us in many colors and attributes, as it pleased him. Who are we to say one color is less or greater than the other?

We were near Hollywood and adjacent cities and noticed some people often felt free from restraint and indulged in eccentric behavior. It seemed normal and totally acceptable. For example: one night, Steve Allen, a television host, had cameras hidden in the Hollywood Farmer's Market. The purpose being, to watch the reaction of the customers to a man dressed as a vampire.

He slithered back and forth throughout the market, his black cape under his nose covering his mouth and chin, his back hunched over in a stooped position, looking cunning from side to side. The people didn't even notice him. They didn't laugh, raise their eyebrows or look around to see if anyone else saw the same thing. They just moved around him continuing their shopping. This revealed the attitude of some in and around Hollywood.

I felt completely out of my comfort zone. I keenly missed, almost ached, for the South. I missed the old oak trees with its moss blowing in the breeze. I loved the parks which divided the blocks where unique small shops were housed. I longed for home, my familiar place. When

I felt lonely or depressed, I would drive to Isle of Hope on the river. There was just something about being there which soothed me.

This lifestyle wasn't what I wanted for myself or my children. I liked the genteel manner of the southern people. It was part of me. We laugh at the intimation that what we say isn't completely honest; certainly it isn't blunt and harsh as the complete honest truth often is. I was southern and had to keep reminding myself, that the Lord wanted us here for whatever his reason. I felt more adaptable and least resistant as I applied myself to reading the Bible and praying often.

Once more, I struggled to settle in my heart and mind, this is where we were to be and God had his purpose. His will be done, not mine.

Chapter 7

Learning To Love

After a few weeks, we found a large upstairs apartment on Ridgley Drive. It had a Spanish décor and was in a pleasant neighborhood. When we moved into this house sized apartment, I was very comfortable. We didn't have a washing machine which I thought was a necessity, but eventually found it was indeed a luxury since there wasn't a stream flowing nearby with large rocks to beat my clothes upon. After a few times of washing my laundry in the bathtub with an old timey washboard like my Grandmother had, my knuckles were scraped raw. Drying was another luxury. There was an umbrella clothesline in the backyard where I could hang my wash until I was told they didn't want us to use it. This reaffirmed what I was thinking about my neighbor's opinion, and the Beverly Hillbilly thing. We began using the Laundromat around the corner.

We didn't have any furniture, but the apartment was partially furnished. I wondered what the elderly landlords who lived downstairs were thinking about tenants who were without furniture. They knew we had traveled across the country and were new to California. Personally, I would have been a little apprehensive.

Robin and I had to walk with Eddie to school. Robin often complained her legs hurt due to the long distance up and down the hilly sidewalks. Harry, as coarse as he was, had a soft heart, especially toward Robin. He bought a wagon in which to pull her. I also used the wagon to take my clothes to and from the Laundromat.

Before we left Savannah, our pastor told us to find a church home as quickly as possible. That advice was wise because it made us feel more stable and connected to a Christian community, although we never really bonded.

It was a pretty little church in Hollywood, and the ministers were warm and caring. He worked with Billy Graham's teams when they were in the city for meetings. I had heard Robert Young, the actor, was a member, but I never saw him.

We attended a Bible class at our church where everyone participated. I listened carefully but couldn't understand what they were saying. This frustrated me and I decided to read the Bible. I had promised the Lord, I would do that while I was in Savannah when I felt I failed him and my neighbor by my ignorance. I knew I would understand it now after sharing the scriptures with our friends.

I opened my white *Bible* which Big Ed had given me, to the book of St. Matthew, and began reading. I immediately became dissatisfied when I bumped into the "begets." I was so determined, I jumped over them and continued reading. I understood and recognized some of what I was reading. I was delighted to find this familiar ground. Then all of a sudden, I read something I had never heard before. From then on, wherever I went, my Bible went. When I washed my dishes, it was propped up in front of me. When I ironed, it was propped up where I could read it. This marvelous book became a part of me. I believed what I read. Jesus was talking directly to me. I was reading about my new life and could see the profile of my wonderful heavenly Father standing by me as his shadow fell upon my shoulders. Before I knew him, this one scripture always seemed to resound in my mind: "Love the Lord your God with all your heart and with all your soul and with your entire mind. This is the first and greatest commandment." [12]

Before my experiencing God personally, this had been frustrating to me. How do you love someone you don't know? I could honor and respect God but love is something else. I needed to have an intimate relationship to love with that passion. Not only that, this is the first and

---

12 Matthew 22:37

great commandment. If I couldn't keep the first commandment, how could I go any further?

Now I knew him. I met God when I gave my life to God's only begotten son, Jesus. Now as I read the *Bible,* I was getting insight into God's likes and dislikes so that I would know how to walk in his love. To know God is to love him and that's the way you love him, with all your heart, soul, mind, body and strength. How blessed we are.

When we arrived for church one Sunday morning, we were told a woman with her five- year- old son had approached the leaders about someone taking them in. She told them she was running away from an abusive husband and needed to hide. She wanted a place to leave her young son and felt he would be safe with a church-going family. She was told to come back that evening. The pastor would share her predicament with the congregation during the morning service and see if there was someone who would be willing to help.

This shocked me because I couldn't imagine any Christian refusing to help. Where did this mother and son sleep last night, I wondered? What if something happened and they couldn't return? Why were they delayed help in such a perilous situation? We are the Lord's people and our hearts and homes should be open to serve at all times.

They made the announcement in church. Stuart and I were in agreement; we told the pastor, we would help them.

That evening the lady with her son came back to church. Her name was Shirley and she told us that she would be all right, but was concerned for Billy, her little boy. She wouldn't accept our invitation for herself. I assured her, we would take good care of him. She said she would send for Billy when she was settled in a place of her own. That was all we knew about her situation. Eddie now had a playmate his own age, and Billy was a member of our family.

I can't remember exactly how long he was with us, but it was a couple of months. Then Shirley came to get him. Even though she had her own place, it was getting late, and we persuaded her to spend the night. It was a Saturday night and before retiring, we were having coffee in our dinette. As we were talking, I felt a wonderful feeling move over my head and shoulders. It was warm and I felt like I was glowing. I looked at Shirley and said, "You are at a crossroad in your life, and you've got to make a decision. It's important you make the right decision for you and your son."

Then the feeling lifted, and I was surprised. I questioned what I had said. I didn't know anything about her except, she was from a Christian home. Where did this knowledge come from?

We all went to church the next morning. When it was time for the altar call, I closed my eyes because it was a holy time. For some reason I opened my eyes and saw Shirley cross in front of me going to the pastor. My impulse was to say, "No, no, you're saved. Why are you going up there?" She told us she was from a Christian home and her father was a minister. Surely, she's saved. I then realized I had assumed she was a Christian just because she was from a Christian home, and this was far from being the truth. The Lord knows everything about us from the inside out. Only the Lord knew her heart, and she was making the decision she was told about the night before. We don't always understand, but the Lord does. He uses us when he chooses, if we let him.

The Lord is so good. I was thankful we obeyed the Lord and his word. It was such a small commitment which would produce such eternal rewards for this small family. We never heard from Shirley or Billy again.

As time passed, we really enjoyed getting together with our new friends, Jay, Lucy, and Ronnie, their son. It was greater than words can express. We read and talked about the Bible. We were learning so much. We shared unimaginable joy and camaraderie. Time would escape us and often, just before daylight, we would leave. I often said laughing as we drove home, "You know we always kept decent hours until we got saved!"

A friend of mine from Florida went to visit us at our Savannah address. A neighbor told her we had moved to Los Angeles. She was shocked. She went home and told her husband. In turn, they decided to sell their home and come out to Los Angeles with us. We told them to come, and I was happy our friends would be sharing in our lives.

Our small family of four, even though we made an effort to be quiet, was a trial for our landlords. Their former tenants were a working couple who were not present during the daytime hours. They didn't have children. Our just being there was bad enough for them to endure, so when our friends with their two children drove up pulling their large trailer, packed with their essentials to begin life in California, it was too difficult even knowing it was temporary until they found their apartment. Now there were eight people living in their upstairs apartment. When the landlords told Stuart we would have to move, it was with an apology. I had never experienced rejection in my life, so this caused me to be disturbed even though I could understand. They were a pleasant couple and I felt like an undesirable person, a new feeling for me.

Before we moved, Harry and Mae, Stuart's sister, came to see us. I was sweeping my porch when they arrived. Being around Harry made me nervous. Before I was aware of what I was doing, I had swept all the way to the public sidewalk and some of it. I stopped sweeping and went into the house.

Harry, in his forward way, asked me, "Tommie, don't you like me?"

I was embarrassed, but in my polite, southern way, I said, "Yes." I don't believe I had even faced my true feelings about Harry because I felt I wasn't giving an honest answer.

On New Year's Eve, we went over to Avis' house. By this time they had moved into a smaller apartment nearer her work. Candles were lit, the house still had decorations from Christmas, and it was a festive time. We stayed only a short time. I was standing near the door waiting for Stuart, so we could leave. Harry was sitting in a chair near the door when all of a sudden, that warm, but this time, heartbreaking feeling came over me. I looked down at Harry and was overcome with such love and compassion, I spontaneously bent over and kissed him on the cheek and said, "I am so sorry, Harry."

Astonished, he asked "For what?"

Blushing, I stammered, "I don't know!" I was overwhelmed, and didn't understand why I had these feelings and moved in such a personal way. I wasn't one to touch others, especially a man. I kissed Harry! What am I going to tell Stuart? I fled to the car. I was so shocked at what I had done.

On our way home, I said, "Honey, I have something to tell you."

"What?"

I struggled for words and finally just said, "I kissed Harry on the cheek. I told him that I was sorry, and I don't know for what!"

"God certainly works in mysterious ways," was all he said.

I thought *yes–well?* Waiting, expecting him to say more that would maybe enlighten me, but on the other hand, I was relieved because I knew for certain it was the Lord's doings once again in my life.

After that, my compassion and love for Harry grew. I never had an ill thought toward him from that day forward. I am the only one who has absolute assurance that he was saved before he passed away, and it's not based on that incident, but another experience I had in prayer a few years later.

In 1971, when we lived in Crete, Illinois, the Lord told me if I would pray for my loved ones as I should, he would save them. I began to earnestly lift our families before God's throne. I was calling each of them by name.

When I prayed for Stuart's family, I was saying, 'Harry's such a hard case, but Avis is hard too. Save Avis, and Harry will believe also."

I was telling God, how to do it and in what order. As I was fervently praying, the Lord interrupted me with a rebuke, *"Is My arm shortened that it cannot save?"* [13]

I hushed quickly hearing his tone. He then said, *"I will save Harry, yet so as by fire.14*

All of Stuart's family eventually were saved and love the Lord to this day. I know beyond a shadow of a doubt that Harry is saved. God is so wonderful.

---

13 Isaiah 59:1
14 1 Corinthians 3:15

Chapter 8

Seek First, What?

I was growing in the Word and in prayer. Once, as I was praying for Stuart's mother, whom I called Mama (her name was Ida), who lived in Chicago, I found myself crying. I didn't understand why I was crying, my heart was deeply moved somewhat like how I had felt toward Harry. My praying, rather than cut and dried methodical words from my mind, was sincere, and there was a depth I had never experienced before. I felt connected with Mama's heart and emotions. My heart was touched and involved, experiencing energy I never had before while praying. It was refreshing in contrast to praying the same old words from my mind and my plan.

I'd heard elder Christians speak of the "spirit of prayer." The Lord knows everything. We need his heart in our prayers. I weep for people I don't know. I feel personally connected to them. Often they become as one of my children. When this happens, I call this God's prayer and God's heart because you will often experience a compassion for one who is unlovely or undeserving of mercy as some would view it. It will be compassion beyond your limits. It will be from God's point of view because He knows the very heart of every human being. We are limited. They won't be experiences to chat about. It's for the prayer closet.

We were still new members in our church when one Sunday before the evening service, the music minister approached me saying, "Sister

Osland, I wonder if you would give your testimony in the service tonight?"

I looked at him blankly wondering, what is a testimony?

Quickly, as if embarrassed, he turned to Stuart and said, "Maybe you could give yours, Brother Osland?"

"I'd be happy to." Stuart replied.

Now I was really puzzled. I knew if Stuart had one, I had one!

After the singing was over, Stuart went up behind the pulpit and told of his experience of finding Jesus for his life.

As I had said previously, Stuart had come to the place in his life where he knew he had not yet received what he needed to live a holy life. Dr. Meadows was a powerful preacher. That particular night at the end of the service, he presented the altar call. The congregation was singing and Stuart's head was bowed. He began to earnestly pray, "Oh, Lord. What do I have to do?" In his own words: "I fell asleep as I stood there. I saw a picture of a silhouette. It was as if I was above this silhouette looking down at this body. It was my body, and it looked like it was full of dirty water, except where my heart was. Then it looked as if someone had pulled a plug and the water started draining out and then my heart was clean and white. Then I awoke and I was standing in the front of the congregation reaching my hand out to Dr Meadows. I wasn't aware of walking down to him as he stood in front of the communion table."

Stuart's testimony was powerful. It was the first time I heard all the details, and I was amazed. He told it just like he experienced it. We thought everyone who was born again experienced finding Jesus as their Savior in similar powerful ways as we had. We still were babies in the religious community. His testimony caused a big stir in the congregation, but we were oblivious to it.

It wasn't long before the ministers asked my husband if we were fellowshipping with "Holiness people?" We didn't know what Holiness people were. I found a tract which was written by someone that had holiness written on it and it asked if we wore shoes with open toes. So I thought Holiness people don't wear toeless shoes. That didn't make much sense to me. The way we were questioned we thought Holiness people, whoever they were, were undesirables, and that puzzled me, also.

We were growing in knowledge as we read and studied the Bible. We were also being challenged in our everyday life to do what we were learning. For instance, when I got saved in Savannah, the first thing the Lord, the Holy Spirit, corrected me about was gossip. At this time, he would now deal with my cigarettes. I knew my mom and dad didn't approve and actually forbade me to do such a thing. Well, you know how those things go. When I was younger I was in a group of teenage girls. We played sports, soft ball, basketball and whatever was available. My mother was the playground director so I was in the park every afternoon.

We had slumber parties. One of the oldest in our group got married and now had her own apartment. We had a party overnight at her house. Everyone in our group smoked except for me. My mother didn't smoke and my parents were strict. That night I was cajoled into smoking. When I yielded, and lit up, I burned a hole in the girl's new tablecloth. I was embarrassed so I determined to learn how to do it correctly. I won't burn any tablecloths! Stupid, huh? I wonder how many stupid situations encourage such an unhealthy habit. Well, in those days, health wasn't even an issue. With my dad, it was: "What if someone sees my daughter smoking?" My dad left his Lucky Strike butts in the ash trays. If I could light them without burning my nose, I collected them, relit them, and blew the smoke out the bathroom window!

Now that I was a grown-up, since Stuart smoked, so could I. Being adults, it was acceptable, except in front of my parents.

We were invited to the home of a family who attended our church. When we arrived, they weren't ready so we sat in their living room waiting. Naturally you must have something to do to pass the time, so we lit up.

I was sitting on the sofa when, all of a sudden, the wife rushed in the living room, hurried to her drapes and began shaking them real hard, making sounds of her disgust.

I was startled because I didn't know what was wrong. She opened the window and stormed back out of the room. I looked for an ash tray, and there wasn't one. Then I realized they weren't smokers, and being embarrassed, I panicked wondering what to do with the butt. Stuart, my darling husband who always managed to save the day, calmly took our cigarette butts outside and discarded them. I began to wonder, could it be that smoking is unacceptable to the Christian community? I don't remember the rest of the visit, personally, I don't think I would have expressed myself in the same manner, but she did get her point across. I knew Christians who smoked. I didn't know that it was a controversial issue, but now I pondered the question.

Mom was a very strong, demanding person. She meant her girls would not smoke. Mother went to my sister's place of work. Linda was sitting at her desk with a cigarette. Mother walked in, I'm certain Linda almost swallowed the cigarette or wished she could. All mother said was, "Linda, I'll see you down in the car."

Linda went down and got in the car. Mother said, "Linda, you have two choices. You can agree never to smoke again or you can eat the rest of the pack of cigarettes."

Like me, she was an adult. But you can guess her choice. She never smoked another cigarette. Mother was Mt. Sinai without a sacrifice. We joke but appreciate her strength to this day. I thanked her many times for her constancy.

When I read in the Bible that my body was the temple (house) of the Holy Ghost, I rubbed my chest thinking, all that smoke, he's probably choking. I now understood there had to be a change. I prayed and refused to smoke. In about three days I had passed the withdrawal period. [15]

Eventually, we moved into a small, less expensive apartment nearby. It wasn't as pretty as the upstairs apartment. Where our new apartment was dark, it was part of an attractive complex with a well-groomed courtyard and surrounding areas. I didn't like the lack of light, but since it provided a sense of being off of a busy street or boulevard, I was able to let the children ride their tricycles on the sidewalks around the courtyard which gave them a sense of freedom. I liked this for them so I could endure the other inconveniences. I also had a relief from being overly concerned about being above our previous landlords. So I felt more relaxed.

It would have been very depressing if my heart was set on having the best. We had actually left our home like missionaries. This wasn't the time for surrounding ourselves with luxuries and dainties. There was a

---

15 1 Corinthians 6:19–20

purpose for all that was happening. We had to focus on the Lord. We were God centered and it wasn't boring, but an exciting adventure.

I will admit it was difficult on the human nature because it doesn't like to hear the word, "No!" It wants pampering and its own way. What made it easy was the Bible. Being filled with God's Word helped. The Bible tells us, "You can't serve God and money." [16]

We are told to "seek those things which are above, which are eternal, not the things which are temporal which will be stolen, and will rust, decay, and which will burn up."[17]

It also tells us, "Where your treasure is, that is where your heart will be."

The key here is the word *serve*. We are told in these scriptures that he is aware you need these things and for we are not to *worry* or be *overly concerned* about them because if we put pleasing him and his kingdom first, he will see that we have the things we need. There are times he will also give us the desires of our heart.

We finally bought a washing machine. I had been washing my linens by hand in a laundry sink with a wooden wash board. God bless those pioneer women! We also purchased a kitchen table with chairs. I bought a few things from the Salvation Army. One thing I particularly remember, an old wooden ironing board. It took a "real woman" to handle that thing! Believe me, when K Mart had a sale on one of those cheap, light ironing board you can guess who was fast getting there? You're right again!

At this time I reached one of my lowest ebb. Our television was repossessed. It wasn't a large expensive console, just a small portable which sat on a small table. I felt so poor. I was ashamed as the employee from a company came to pick it up.

I heard a knock on my door. I opened carefully because I didn't have many visitors being new to the city.

I see a man in a gray uniform. "Yes?"

"Ma'am, I'm with Alpha Credit Company. I have instructions to pick up a television set for them."

"Come in." I lead him to the table.

---

16 Matthew 6:24–33
17 Matthew 6:21

He begins to unplug the set and winds the cord. As he pushes in the antenna, he says, "Ma'am, I'm so sorry. I hate doing this." He moves toward the door.

I follow. "It's all right. Where we are in life, if we have any money, we would have to choose between a loaf of bread and a television payment, the bread would win out." I'm sick at heart and feel defeated. I began to sink in my spirit. I became angry with Stuart who couldn't find a job. In my mind I knew Stuart would do anything within legal boundaries to provide for us, but when darkness comes in with his impressions, he will block out human reasoning. I didn't fight because, as of yet, I wasn't aware of the dark side or spiritual warfare.

When Stuart got home, I told him, "I don't care what you do. Do whatever you like, just see that the children and I have food and a place to live." I felt my marriage was over.

Even after all these years, I hurt in my heart when I remember this time because like everything we experienced we learned how faithful God is to provide for his children. This wasn't an exception. I failed Stuart at this time and he didn't retaliate against me. I wish I could give a glowing miracle here. The only thing I can say is, since there wasn't a television, I began playing music on my record player. Avis, Stuart's sister, had given me some old hymns and I played them over and over. What a blessing they were. Placing them on a scale against each other, I'm certain more faith flowed from them than would have flowed from the television.

Our lives were becoming somewhat more normal except Stuart was still struggling to find a job.

There was a little black girl in Eddie's kindergarten class named Cookie. I met her grandmother who walked to school also. Cookie cried a lot and the teacher told me her mother had gone away to a southern state. Cookie missed her mother terribly. Eddie felt sorry for her and wanted to bring her home with us. I was touched by his compassion, and spoke with her grandmother. She told me Cookie's mother was in Louisiana.

Cookie came home with us one day and had lunch. She and Eddie played together with his toys, and then we took her home at the end of the day. I think Eddie befriending her helped lessen the child's unhappiness. Also, I had never been socially connected to any black people. This was helping to break down walls in my life as well.

Even with all the miracles the Lord was doing in our behalf, there were times I felt drained and tired. At these times, I longed for a mundane life with a job for Stuart and our own home away from a big city. These times weren't very often and were certainly not filled with faith that moved mountains but, while studying the Bible, I saw the heroes of the faith also experienced up and down times.

One Sunday evening during Training Union (This was a class where everyone was given scriptures to read and present the following Sunday. It was like homework.) I was given a scripture. I studied it and when called upon, I read it out loud to the class. Then I commented about what was happening in the church in the book of Acts, God was greatly moving among his people so naturally the church would be successful and grow. Well, it wasn't what they wanted to hear! The people were stunned. Silence fell and fell hard. I wasn't aware these types of services were descriptive of "Holiness churches!" I didn't know what else to say. I had been reading the Bible without guidance or prejudice. It was fresh. I didn't know about men's doctrines, cults and other denominations which were unacceptable because of their differences. Until this time, I thought all true Christians had experienced the Holy Spirit, the same as I had. I was open and hungry for more of him and excited about what he was saying in the Bible. I didn't have difficulty understanding what the Bible was saying. I was having difficulty with what people were saying!

I made friends with the neighborhood butcher in a small meat market on the way to school, and he told me how to fix hamburger to taste like steak. Even hamburger was a luxury. Whenever our food got low, I would become apprehensive, but when we needed something, it always came to our front door without solicitation of any sort. These were difficult times because we had in the past used credit of some sort to fill in the gaps between paydays. Now we were learning to pray, wait and watch. The Lord never failed us.

Christmas was approaching and we didn't have any money. It was heartbreaking to think my babies wouldn't have any presents, and I tried not to think about it. I even considered hiding the fact that it was Christmastime. Early one evening Jay, Lucy and Ronnie surprised us with an unexpected visit. When we opened the door, they came in carrying a live six-foot Christmas tree and a box of decorations. The smell of the fresh tree filled our apartment as we decorated. What color and warmth they brought to our home. How much our friends loved us!

A few days later, two of my friends came to see me and invited me to go to the boulevard for a hot dog. I was embarrassed because I didn't have money. I was going to make an excuse when someone knocked on my door. When I answered, a man I didn't know was standing holding a sheet of paper.

"Mrs. Osland?"

"Yes?"

"You are Mrs. Osland?" he asked again.

"Yes, I am." Now I was curious. He asked me to please wait a minute, he would be right back.

I turned to my friends shaking my head. I was bewildered. I told them I wouldn't be able to go with them and before they could answer, the man returned carrying a big box.

I hadn't ordered anything. My friends just stood there waiting with me to find out what was going on. He went back out the door and I went over to the box to see what was inside. It was full of groceries.

He put another box down and went out again. This happened several times. I was overwhelmed, but what really made me cry was the last box. It was full of Christmas gifts.

I asked, "Who–?"

He interrupted me, "I'm sorry. I cannot disclose who sent these things. I was told to tell you to have a very merry Christmas." And he left. Every time I think about this, I still cry.

My friends were taken aback and I was struggling, trying not to cry. They left quickly and then, I just let my tears flow while thanking the Lord with all my heart. My children would have a Christmas after all and so would we! If you are ever blessed to minister to people in this way, please don't forget the bathroom necessities. Before this time, I would never have thought of them. These provisions were also included in one of the boxes. How thoughtful the gift givers had been.

These were humbling times. We learned God uses people. He blessed those who had been so generous for their obedience, who gave in our time of need. You have to learn to receive as well as give. The saying, *It is easier to give than receive,* is true, but we need to realize that this is often the way it happens. Be gracious; be thankful, this is the Lord's way. [18]

In my past, during my senior year at high school, I was in typing class, someone behind me asked, "What motto do you want in the annual?"

I didn't have a motto! I was busy typing, and the teacher was timing us, but I replied, "Seek ye first the kingdom of God and all these things shall be added unto you."

I was busy, so I forgot about this incident until several years later, just before the Lord healed Eddie when we lived at Thunderbolt, someone from my graduation class called to remind me of our reunion. I took out my annual to show Stuart the person who had called. That's when I saw my motto printed under my picture and I was shocked, I didn't go to church or read the Bible when I was in school. So, *where did this knowledge come from?* I didn't even understand what it meant?

Years later in California, while we were learning to lean on the Lord for our needs, it was as if a big piece of puzzle fell into its correct position. We were beginning to understand what that scripture meant. Our life was forming a picture, and it continues to this day. We do serve a living and exciting God.

---

18 Luke 6:38

Chapter 9

Tasting of the Heavenly Gift

I sensed Stuart's family distancing themselves from us. When we visited them, there seem to be coldness. They brought out the religious books and discussion would begin about religion. We never instigated these discussions. We shared our experience coupled with what the Bible had to say when we first arrived. Afterwards, we just waited for the Lord to show them. We wanted to be part of the family even though we didn't seem to have any common interests. They were Stuart's family, and this made me sad

We were enjoying wonderful fellowship with Jay, Lucy and Ronny. My knowledge of the Bible was growing and I basked in the reality of God's promises.

One memorable evening at Jay's house, he and I were sitting at the table in the dining room and as he read from the *Bible*, I followed reading from mine:

"*Now to each one the manifestation of the Spirit is given for the common good. To one there is given through the Spirit the message of wisdom, to another the message of knowledge by means of the same Spirit, to another faith by the same Spirit, to other gifts of healing by that one Spirit, to another miraculous powers, to another prophecy, to another distinguishing between spirits, to another speaking in different kinds of tongues, and to still another the interpretation of tongues. All these are the work of one and the same Spirit, and he gives them to each one, just as he determines."* 19

At this point I stopped him. "Jay, what are *tongues?*"

He paled, and solemnly explained. "The *tongues* spoken of are unlearned languages of various kinds given as gifts by the Holy Spirit to Believers. During church services someone might speak in one of these languages, but unless there was an interpreter present, they were not to speak. The one who spoke in this unknown language was to pray they themselves would be enabled to interpret what was being spoken in the particular language; otherwise in the church they were to keep silent. There was a limit on such speaking. Two and at the most, three were to be allowed to speak. Also it is written in the Bible, "*For he who speaks in a tongue does not speak to men but to God, for no one understands him; however, in the spirit he speaks mysteries."* 20

"I've never heard about anything like this. This doesn't happen in my church, why not?" I asked.

Jay looked down, chuckled and said, "I can't tell you."

I could tell he was relieved our conversation was almost over.

"Do things like that happen in churches today?"

"Yes, they do."

"That I've got to see!" I told him. Now my curiosity was piqued.

I went home and immersed myself into the Bible. I read and re-read from Matthew to Revelation. I decided, if Stuart agreed, I would not return to our church, nor would I attend one like Jay said existed today with the manifestations we discussed. My church would naturally say, "This is not for us today, based on the fact it wasn't in practice." The other would say, "Oh, yes. This is for us today."

I knew this would cause me distress. After all, hadn't the Lord come to my house and directed me what to do? He would meet me again and let me know what to do now. I would obey the Lord.

The following Sunday, Stuart went to church without me. I felt lonely and I missed church. Since getting saved, Sunday had changed from being a miserable day to being the highlight of my week.

The children stayed home with me and we were in the living room on the bed. We only had one bedroom; we had a day bed in our living

---

19 1 Corinthians 12:7–11
20 1 Corinthians 14:2

room. We were watching a church service and as the minister prayed for someone who was sick, I bowed my head and prayed also. To my delight the warm Holy Spirit of the Lord filled my living room and surrounded me. I didn't expect this to happen. This let me know that God wasn't restricted to a church building during church time. [21]

I didn't feel alone after this. When Stuart came home from church, he had a book the pastor had given him. It explained from their point of view, why they decided these things had passed away and was not for us today.

I hesitated, but finally read it. The primary scripture they used was:

"Charity never faileth, but whether there be prophecies, they shall fail; whether there be tongues, they shall cease; whether there be knowledge, it shall vanish away. For we know in part, and we prophesy in part. But when that which is perfect is come, then that which is in part shall be done away." [22]

They said the *perfect* which was to come was the *Bible*. Since we now had the *Bible*, these spiritual gifts were not necessary, but were only used to start the church.

Shortly after reading the book, I went to the Lord and asked him to settle this for me. To move on in my life, I needed to know where to worship. I didn't like not having a church, and continued reading and studying daily.

Six weeks passed and late one night, I would soon close my *Bible* and go to bed, when I realized my stopping place was 1 Corinthians 13:8. I became discouraged. It seemed like it had been a long time since I asked Him for this answer. I was tired from the long day. I slumped in my chair frustrated when unexpectedly, I felt his warmth around my body, and I knew**,** once again He gave me *the gift of knowledge*: *When that which is perfect is come,* when *Jesus returns, we won't need these gifts.* Everything will be complete.

We need the gifts, the genuine gifts from the Holy Ghost, now. They were for now. They were for me and *Jesus' Church*. We need the same power and how much more so in the last days? We have the same grace that saves us and God the Father, Son and Holy Ghost never

---

21 Isaiah 66:1

22 1 Corinthians 13:8–10

changes. If we are to be *the Church*, we need the empowerment that will help us stand and excel for God's glory.

Once again, I surrendered everything to God. I laid my ambition, my desires, and my family; I laid everything on the altar. Jesus would truly be my first love. I said to Jesus, "If you will fill me with your Holy Spirit, I will speak when and wherever you want me to speak, but I must have the empowerment of the Holy Spirit to be this kind of witness."

From that moment, I waited expectantly for the answer to this prayer. I knew it was the Lord's desire for me.

In my study of the scriptures, I saw the blessing of the baptism of the Holy Spirit. As a born again Believer, I knew the Holy Spirit was inside my body, which was his temple, otherwise I was none of his.

"You, however, are controlled not by the sinful nature but by the Spirit, if the Spirit of God lives in you. And if anyone does not have the Spirit of Christ, he does not belong to Christ." [23]

I saw where to be filled with and controlled by the Holy Spirit was indeed a baptism of power to be a witness for Jesus. I also read about the gifts the Holy Spirit gives as it pleases Him. I read in the book of Acts where these gifts were in operation in the Believers.

I continued my studies seeking deeper knowledge and insight about the Holy Spirit. I lived expecting the answer to my prayer.

I read and heard of many receiving this blessing and power from the outpouring of the Holy Spirit a few years ago. I had never heard such things before. I knew my Lord loved me and to completely fill me with the Holy Spirit would be glorious and I would be a powerful witness to the world in which I lived. Every evening before I went to sleep, I would tell the Lord that I believed this promise was for me and I believed I would receive it that very night. After awhile, this seemed redundant, but I still spoke the words as I finished praying.

Several weeks passed and after an evening spent in fellowship with Jay and Lucy we returned home well after midnight. We had gone to bed and as I was praying, I felt something begin to move in the midsection of my body. There wasn't any pain. The only time I ever experienced anything like this was when I was pregnant.

---

23 Romans 8:9

This movement slowly began to move upward, and as it reached my lungs, it felt like my ribs pulled apart. My chest was filled with this fullness, and then my neck until this sensation exited my mouth. There wasn't any sound. This continued over and over until I heard water fall heavily in a splattering sound. Everyone was sound asleep. I wondered what this all meant.

Then the Lord's voice spoke and said, "Out of the belly will flow rivers of living waters." [24]

The movement continued and water kept falling until I thought, I really need to check my sinks to make sure.

When I stood up the movement stopped and I didn't hear the water falling anymore. Everything ceased as I went into the kitchen and then, the bathroom. There wasn't any water running. I went back to bed and as soon as I lay down, the movement and the water falling started again, continuing until I fell asleep.

From that time on, when I thought about the Lord or scriptures, the Holy Spirit would move inside my body. I likened this time to a tea kettle. It's simplistic, I know, but it seemed like pressure would build up inside my body without ability to vent it. There was no release.

One evening Jay and Lucy were going to San Bernardino to a small Pentecostal church. They invited me to go with them. It was small and the people were friendly. I felt comfortable, at least until they started singing. The singing was good, but they clapped their hands. I had never been in a church where there was clapping.

I became uncomfortable, so I prayed. "Lord, I know you and you know me, but I'm not sure about these people." I couldn't leave so I randomly opened my *Bible*. My eyes fell immediately on *"Oh, clap your hands, all you peoples! Shout to God with the voice of triumph! For the LORD Most High is awesome; He is a great King over all the earth."* 25

This is a good thing. It's what the Lord wants us to do, I decided. Gingerly I began to clap. I discovered it wasn't disrespectful after all. Soon I was relaxed and enjoying the service. I began to tremble even though I wasn't cold.

I whispered to Lucy, "I'm not cold!"

---

24 John 7:37–38
25 Psalms 47:1

Lucy saw how I was shaking. In her Italian way, she lifted her hands and shouted, "Stop the church! The Lord wants to fill Tommie with the Holy Ghost."

I was taken back at her doing this because, in church, she was always quiet and stayed in the background.

The next thing I knew I was being led by people down to an altar where I got down on my knees. I had just adjusted to clapping when everyone began to pray out loud over and around me. By this time, I wasn't shaking and realized they were enthusiastically expecting the Lord to fill me.

I had been waiting for some time privately and was a bit discouraged. If the Lord had told me to stand on my head to receive this blessing, I would have tried to do so. Now here I was in the middle of a bunch of strangers who were praying loudly over me! I felt like I had to produce the golden egg and knew I couldn't. I was crying in my heart and all I could say over and over was, "Oh, Lord!" but in my heart I was saying, I wish I was home. With my mouth I was groaning a sincere prayer saying, "Oh, Lord!" It wasn't very long before my words turned into being one and the same prayer, with my heart. I felt joy filling my chest as the sadness left me, and I was worshipping the Lord. Then something strange began to happen to my mouth as I was saying, "Oh, Lord." It felt like a small electrical wire was attached to the outside of my tongue. My "Oh, Lord" began to sound different. It was unintelligible. My tongue was supercharged and took on a movement all its own. I began to stammer and sounds emerged from my spirit.

Everyone began to shout praises to the Lord. I was worshipping the Lord with all my heart and I didn't care about anything. In fact, I didn't give a thought to anyone except my Lord. The tea kettle now had a spout to release its steam. I was experiencing a complete, total release in my spirit. There isn't anything which can compare with this experience in this world.

Just before leaving that little church, two different ladies at two separate times came to me and said I would have a ministry where people would confide personal information about themselves to me and I wasn't to share this information with anyone. They also told me, I would be used in Intercessory Prayer. This happened forty-five years ago and has been true. So far this is the way the Lord has primarily used me.

On the drive home, I felt like I was glowing. I had deep satisfaction and happiness. I had total contentment. The Lord had greatly blessed me and I was prepared for his service. I felt complete. I could understand Mary's adoration of the Lord when she exclaimed to her cousin, Elizabeth, "And Mary said, My soul doth magnify the Lord, And my spirit hath rejoiced in God my Saviour." *26*

---

26 Luke 1:46–47

Chapter 10

A Glistening White Robe

One of the first miracles the Holy Spirit did through me in ministering to someone with the laying on of hands challenged me by some of the ways I had been taught as a youth. A few months after arriving in Los Angeles, we joined an Interdenominational church. We were singing in a choir of one hundred which ministered on radio and television. The choir was a praying group well known for its serious ministry, and we were learning how God could move a group by the anointing of his Holy Ghost.

The members came from far and near; one member even flew in from Arizona for choir practice and services. We saw many people receive Christ and experience various miracles which included healings and deliverance from demon possession.

During an evening service, our choir director motioned for me to go down to the altar and pray with someone. I had never prayed for anyone other than my children. As I walked around the corner of the piano, I saw a black lady kneeling at the altar.

I gasped; I'd never touched a person of color other than my nanny. Having a conversation in public is one thing, but touching was another! Strange how things you are taught as a young child can hold you prisoner. It took only seconds for me to realize what was happening. I rejected those barriers, and was free to pray for my sister.

I got on my knees, facing her, and asked, "Sister is there something I can pray with you about?"

"I just came down here to ask the pastor to pray for me." she replied.

I was relieved! "Wait a minute. I'll be right back." I got up and headed for the podium where our pastor was standing. I took only a few steps when *the Holy Spirit* spoke emphatically, "*The Believer shall! The Believer shall! The Believer shall!*" [27]

I was a Believer and I was to pray. As I turned, I was filled with the Holy Spirit. I don't remember walking to her, but only remember being back on my knees saying, "I'll pray for you!"

When I placed my hands on her shoulders, an electric current filled me from the top of my head to the bottom of my feet. I felt the pores in my hands open as the current went through them out into her body. The power going through me was so strong it was all I could do to remain on my knees, but since the power was leaving my hands and entering her, I knew I must keep my hands on her. This was one of the most powerful experiences I have ever had in my life.

During our next service that evening on the radio, the pastor asked the lady to stand and tell the congregation what her problem had been. She said she had a goiter and it was gone. She was healed.

I wonder what would have happened if I had succumbed to my upbringing?

At choir practice a couple of weeks later a young, single mother who was a college student facing her final exam, stood to give testimony. She had been fearful of failing because this education had cost her so much time and expense, and she had to work to support herself and her child. The previous night when she went before the Lord in prayer, she said she felt the Lord lifting her up before him. He said, "Do not fear. I will be with you, and you will not fail." Weeping, she told us she now had peace about her upcoming exam.

I had never heard such a thing. He would bless me like this as I prayed? My prayer time changed immensely. I began to look forward to praying in my closet. I realized that the promise Jesus gave of my Father seeing me in secret and rewarding me openly was truly a reality. [28]

---

27 Mark 16:15–20
28 Matthew 6:6

I had received the Baptism of the Holy Spirit, and I expected the Holy Spirit to flow freely through me; he didn't. He still moved inside my body, but not overflowing like I had experienced in that little church, and nothing had changed in my daily life to hinder his freedom.

One day while I was working in my kitchen, I started singing, *"This is my story, this is my song, praising my Savior all the day long."* I felt the warmth of the Holy Spirit surrounding me. I was exhilarated and reaching notes easily with a full, rich volume. I knew something was happening as I continued worshipping in song. Then I heard some noise. It was coming from the kitchen in the upstairs apartment. My Jewish landlord was working upstairs. The Lord was ministering to my landlord as I sang. I continued worshipping and thanking God in my heart for this blessed time.

One evening Jay and Lucy came for a visit. We sat in the kitchen having coffee and sharing about our recent week. Jay never could just sit and talk, but would inevitably, stand and preach. This time was always wonderful.

It was a warm night and all our windows were open to let in a breeze. I saw a vision. As Jay preached, his words were written on a banner which was flowing out of the window. I kept still and didn't say anything, fearing we would lose the moment.

Near midnight, we joined hands and stood in a circle in the living room for our parting prayer. We took turns praying whatever was on our hearts. Suddenly, the Holy Spirit filled me like a volcano erupting with great power and volume. My spirit sang in a high soprano voice where normally, I was alto or second soprano. Then after awhile (the length of time was immeasurable) I began to speak in four different languages. I didn't understand what I was saying, but I was greatly edified. I was aware of my surroundings but unaware of what was happening to anyone else.

I heard a knock and my husband answered the door. Stuart told us later that when he opened the door, two policemen were there. One of the policemen inquired if everything was all right.

Stuart explained we were praying when the Holy Spirit fell upon us, and we were worshipping God.

The black officer pulled on the back of the white officer's shirt saying, "I know what these people are saying and we need to leave them alone."

The policeman said, "Sir, if you will just close your window, it would help."

Afterward, I felt bad about the police being called. I had never experienced any problem with the authorities in my life. This was such a wonderful spiritual experience; I didn't care at that time what else was happening. Later, Lucy shared with me that she was seeing visions. I never asked what she saw.

When Jay and his family left our apartment, he said the courtyard was full of people from various cultures. He was carrying his *Bible* and with a smile, nodded a greeting as they went to their car.

However, the mother of our landlord was very angry and insisted her son evict us immediately. He refused, saying, "They are worshipping God, and I won't interfere."

The next time we were with Jay and Lucy, I said, "We need to find a house instead of an apartment if things like these are going to happen."

We again stood in our prayer circle and petitioned the Lord for a home. Lucy asked specifically that it would have a large front and back yard, fenced in for the children. In my heart, I laughed. Imagine in a city of asphalt and concrete, a large yard for my children. I laughed because it was unreal that she would even ask.

Guess what? Yes, that's exactly what we received. I knew the Lord had answered Lucy's prayer for us a home when I saw the size of the yards and the backyard was even fenced in. It was a remodeled house located in East Los Angeles. We were not on the boulevard but a side street adjoining it. It was in walking distance to grocery stores, banks, and various shops. I took advantage of these conveniences since I didn't drive anymore.

Since our neighborhood consisted primarily of Mexicans, I found it would have been easier if I knew Spanish. Since I didn't speak Spanish as we walked to the boulevard, big smiles and a wave of the hand had to suffice. As in most large cities, people were more private than in the south. At first they just stared at us curiously but after a time, they returned our smiles and waved back.

One day I took Robin and we walked to the bank. The door was locked so I thought we were too early. I knew it wouldn't be long so we patently waited by the door. Suddenly, police cars zoomed up at all angels with the front of their cars all pointing toward us. A crowd began to gather, everyone excitedly speaking in Spanish and I was in the dark except for my imagination. The police jumped out of their cars and I moved back as they ran past me and Robin and into the bank. I took Robin and we went inside the drug store next door. Eventually I learned the bank had been robbed while Robin and I were standing outside the bank's door. It was an unnerving experience. Spanish is a very important language for Americans to learn today.

Another example for this is, there was a garage apartment behind us facing the next street. One day I met a precious five year old girl, named Carla. She had shoulder length brown hair with green eyes that danced as she spoke.

"Know what?"

"No, Carla, what?"

"My Mommy was gonna have two babies."

"She was?"

"Yeah. But the nurses killed em."

"Oh, my. Carla, is that true?"

"Yeah! Mommy said so. And the doctor! And we don't have any babies, anymore"

"I'm so sorry." I was shocked by what she said so I didn't continue our conversation. She played with the children and I went indoors.

I made it a point to visit with Harry's mother Juana who lived down on the corner house. She was walking the baby when I told her about mine and Carla's conversation. She told me that Carla's parents couldn't speak English.

"Juana, will you go tell them what Carla thinks so they can talk with her? If they had to take her or go themselves to the doctor or hospital, she would be upset."

"Well, I don't know if they will understand me. There are different ways to speak Spanish."

"Will you try? Children often get fragments of information and it gets distorted. We assume they know all that is necessary and just take them along with us without explaining the details on their level of understanding. Their little eyes gather the sights they see and put the details together the best they can."

"Okay, I'll try."

I could tell the way she was acting she didn't want to do it.

Juana then told me, Carla's father brought a fellow worker home for supper. When supper was ready to be served, her mother spoke in Spanish to him. The man didn't understand what she had said so Carla told him, "Mother says you are dirty and need a bath before you can eat at the table." Juana began to laugh and I just shook my head.

As she walked away, she could tell I was disturbed. She stopped, looked at me and said, "All right, I'll go and see her. Maybe she'll understand what I am saying."

"Thank you. At least we can try and help."

*   *   *

We didn't know East Los Angeles was a dangerous place to live because of the drug situation. We had an old house next to us on our right and a small old house on our left on the far back of the property, but to our left beginning at the public sidewalk extending to the back corners of our house was a newer duplex apartment. The front apartment near the sidewalk was large. Our landlord and his family lived there and the adjoining small back apartment had someone else living in it.

Jay and Lucy had provided us with a house full of furniture they had in storage. We were closer to them but further from our church. We were having car trouble, and until Stuart repaired the car, they would come and give us a ride to church.

One evening, Stuart went to choir practice, leaving me and the children alone. I never liked being alone at night. I was watching television in our back room when I heard some noise. I got up and started into the kitchen when I thought it's just my imagination, so I went back and sat down.

The next morning my landlord told me there had been a gang fight in my drive-way. Since I didn't have a phone, she couldn't call me. She and the neighbor on the other side of us were talking on their phones and peeping out their windows. There was a stabbing and the gang scattered leaving the victim in my driveway. However, when Stuart got home, he couldn't tell anything had happened.

When Jay and Lucy invited me to go with them to a new church, I eagerly accepted. It was a large church with an overflowing congregation. We enjoyed it so much we decided to go back the following week. The mail came as I was ironing and I was ready for a break. It was a letter from my mother, and I sat down. Opening the letter, I began to read. It wasn't long before I felt a knot tightening in my stomach. She told me five Baptist ministers visited with her, and advised her not to allow me to correspond with my sister. If a letter came, she was to read it and then, after scanning it, let Bobbie have it. They also said, the experience I had received came from the devil, not God.

The tightening in my stomach was so hard, while reading the letter, I couldn't sit up. I bent over and began to groan. When the tightening relaxed and the groaning lifted, I was weeping. I said to the Lord, "Oh, God. Five ministers and five churches misled. Fill them with the Holy Spirit and make them speak in tongues from their pulpits!" I understood later, I had been, what is called in the Full Gospel churches, *travailing in the Spirit.* Afterward, although sick in heart, I felt better and resumed my ironing.

As I left to go with Jay and Lucy, I tucked the letter in my pocket to share with them so they would pray. We sat on a pew near the back and when the time came for testimonies, I began to tremble. It came to me to stand and share the letter with the congregation. I knew it was what the Lord wanted. Afterwards, I sat down, a lady about four rows from the front stood, under the anointing of the Holy Ghost. When the anointing lifted and she could speak, she said she had been in intercession on my behalf that morning for several hours. The Lord told her he was going to answer the prayer I had prayed.

Later, the Lord revealed the truth about the Baptism of the Holy Spirit to my mother; she asked in a letter, "Why don't they (her denomination) teach us about the Holy Spirit?" I told her, "The last quarterly I read before leaving that denomination, the lesson was titled, "The Holy Spirit." In the lesson, they admitted not understanding much about him."

After we moved into this house a division came between Jay, Lucy and ourselves. It was such a sharp division it couldn't be resolved by discussion. We went over to try and talk with them, but they weren't home. I wrote letters, but they weren't answered. The only thing left to do was pray, and we had been doing that. This caused me deep grief. I loved them dearly.

I was lonely. I found myself going into the closet to pray more often. This is where I discovered my prayer closet and really learned to pray. The closet in this house was a larger than the average closet but smaller than a walk-in. Our clothes hung on one side so I could sit with my back against the wall with my knees drawn up. If it was a lengthy time and sometimes it was, I would shift positions to be comfortable.

Eddie was now in school for a full day and my daughter, Robin, played with her toys so I had extra time to read, and pray.

As I drew closer to God, God drew closer to me and I came to know him better. The *Bible* tells us: "Draw nigh to God, and he will draw nigh to you." [29]

His promise after I surrendered my life to him was "I'll not let anyone hurt you again," became a reality. When I would hurt I would go to him and he would lift the hurt from me. It's just like slipping a dress off over my head. Along with this, when I sensed any dissatisfaction or unusual feeling or emotion; I would go to my prayer closet and pray, even though I didn't know who it was for or the basis for these feelings. If I was distressed, I would cry, groan and let my emotions out. Many times I would just vent my feelings until they actually turned into laughter. I prayed until I had peace. Most of the time, I talked to the Lord out loud. Sometimes I sat silently knowing he was there. Jesus told me, the Father would see me. If it happened in the middle of the night or even the wee hours of the morning, I would slip out of bed and move into my closet next to my bed. It was never a chore, but a delight. When the dark emotion lifted, the Lord's presence comforted me. Here I learned how and when to respond to his leading.

Eddie was down the street at his bud Harry's house and Robin was next door playing in the neighbor's garage with the little girl and boy who lived there. I was busy cleaning the house when I heard the front door slam. I went to the living room to see who it was because the children generally didn't come home until I called. It was Robin and she was crying.

---

29 James 4:8a

"What's wrong?" I asked as I put my arms around her.

"Where was he, Mama?"

"Where was who?"

"You said that we had angels that helped us when we got hurt. Why didn't he stop Jimmy from pulling me down the sidewalk by my hair? I called, but he didn't help me?" She began to sob.

Robin had long, silky, blond hair. It was easy to grab if someone wanted to hurt her, and that was what the little neighbor boy had done. Robin was a gentle soul, and only helped people. She never hurt anyone.

I was devastated. I taught the children from the *Bible* to instill faith in our loving God. I believed what I taught them, and they received it. I was their mother, and wouldn't teach them a lie. I soothed and made her comfortable, but I didn't have an answer. As soon as I felt I could leave her, I hurried to pray.

I literally burst into the closet, fell on my knees releasing the emotions I had hidden from my baby girl. My head was down, and all I could say was, "Oh, God," I sobbed over and over. Also I said, "I believe. Why?"

My prayer closet was dark, but I always saw little glimmers of lights popping here and there, like little Christmas tree lights blinking, only smaller. I thought, it was just my eyes adjusting to the dark.

As my crying subsided, calm settled over me, and the little lights were flashing. Peace filled my closet as the lights became more numerous and larger. I felt like I was being held, and I became still and quiet. My head was down as it was when I was praying, and my eyes were open. Slowly, the lights became so large, they joined together and formed a long glistening white robe which fell in folds touching the closet floor. I could see about shin high, but I couldn't lift my head any higher. Holiness filled my closet. I don't know how long I remained in that position, I didn't want to move because I was filled with such peace and awe; I stayed still, basking in the overwhelming *Holiness*.

Holiness: There isn't an adequate word to describe it. *Holiness* surrounds our heavenly Father. He emits *holiness*. "It is written: 'But as he which hath called you is holy, so be ye holy in all manner of conversation; because it is written, be ye holy; for I am holy.' " [30]

---

30 1 Peter 1:15–16

The only way to be holy is to spend time with him in his presence.

After Moses spent the time with God receiving the Ten Commandments, he descended from the mountain, his face glowed and the people were frightened.

We don't spend time with God in our prayer closets, and come out the same as we entered. We are *changed* from glory to glory. "But we all, with open face beholding as in a glass the glory of the Lord, are changed into the same image from glory to glory, even as by the Spirit of the Lord." [31]

Many people think spending time in prayer is unproductive since we can't show something tangible that comes from this time. Much of what happens between oneself and the Lord begins there. [32]

We need to forget our ambition and goals, snuggle up to him, and receive his directions when he's ready to give them. Otherwise we just "delight ourselves in the Lord." [33]

There won't be too many trips to the closet before your cup will be full.

I never received an answer to give Robin, but I did share with her about what happened in the closet.

---

31   2 Corinthians 3:18
32   John 15:5
33   Psalms 37:4

Chapter 11

An Unwelcomed Intruder

Living in our area, along the boulevard were taco stands advertising green chili, red chili and all varieties of delicious Mexican foods. I cultivated a taste for most of them to a certain degree, and I do mean-degree!

When Juana had a birthday celebration for Harry, it included all the parents. Stuart was working so I went with Eddie and Robin. A complete Mexican dinner from scratch was served. Oh, how delicious it was. I enjoyed every bite, but, not being used to the spices, the following two days, I felt like something terrible had taken place, such as an explosion. In my mouth, it was delicious, but oh, afterwards!

Our living room window was on the side of our house. As I looked out the window I could see the bathroom window of the apartment next door. Often at two in the morning, I would be awakened by sounds of someone regurgitating in the bathroom. I never saw the occupant, but I thought it was a man, and I would lie in my bed and pray for him as he was throwing up. I felt a connection to him due to my prayers.

After a few months, things to do for the Lord seemed to be at a standstill, and I began to doubt if we were still living in the right neighborhood. When I was in my closet, I asked the Lord for confirmation that we were in the right place, or if we should relocate.

During this time, while praying, I became uneasy about Eddie. He was down at Harry's house, and I felt an urgency to check on him.

I left my house and hurried across the front lawn. I reached the sidewalk and strained to see if I could hear the boys. Everything was quiet, so I began to walk briskly toward Harry's house. I had only taken a few steps when a passing car suddenly slammed on brakes and backed quickly at an angle against the curb near where I was walking. It startled me and I stopped and moved backwards. A man was driving and a lady was sitting beside him in the front seat. He leaned over her and called to me from her open window. I moved closer to hear what he was saying but not so near that I could be grabbed.

"You're a Christian, aren't you?"

Stunned, I answered, "Yes. I am." I didn't know these people!

He said, "I knew it! I'm your neighbor. I live in the back apartment next door. I'm a minister and have cancer. I'm backslidden."

Realizing this was God's doings, I moved closer to the car saying, "God is in the same place where you left him. He loves you and can heal you."

"What? Come back and let him put something else on me?"

"God didn't put that on you. I'll pray for you."

Suddenly, the lady beside him began to cry. "I'm backslidden, too. Please pray for me, too."

I told her that I would.

As suddenly as they had stopped, they drove away leaving me trembling and speechless. This was a dramatic answer to the prayer I had just prayed. We were indeed in the place where the Lord wanted us. My anxiousness over Eddie was from the Holy Spirit. He wanted me to go to the sidewalk at that same time they would be passing in the car.

Later I learned Ben had been a minister of a church and had strayed off into false doctrine. This seduction cost him his church, reputation and family. I tried to get him to go to a service and be prayed for, but he declined. I didn't see much of him. Every now and then, if I found something inspiring for him to read; I took it to him.

One day while I was over near Ben's apartment, I heard someone moving around inside. I knocked on the door. A young woman answered. I was surprised, then concerned. I introduced myself and asked about Ben.

She told me she was his daughter. She thanked me for being there for her daddy and said, "He asked me to come and give you a message. 'He said to tell you that he and the Lord had talked, and he was ready to go home to be with Him.' He had passed away.

I thanked her for giving me his message, and I wept as I went to my house. God is so full of mercy and love for His children.

A few days later it was Robin's birthday and we planned a special party. We had a garage next to our house. It had a window on the back wall which was perfect for what we had planned. There was a popular TV series where they used puppets. Stuart arranged the set for the puppet show using Mr. Do Bee which was a hand puppet designed as a colorful bee. After the party we had to make the children go home. They didn't want to leave. Early the following morning I heard something outside my back door. When I looked out, there was a little guy calling, "Mr. Do Bee! Mr. Do Bee!" I had to take him back home. I knew the party had been a big success.

One morning the children and I slept late since school was out, and we were a little slow starting our day. We dressed and were beginning our devotions when someone knocked on the door. It was Harry.

"Eddie will be out in just a few minutes, okay?"

"Okay."

I closed the door and resumed my reading when I thought, let Harry come inside and be with you.

"Wait just a minute, kids."

"Harry." I called.

"Yeah?"

"Would you like to come in and have devotions with us?"

"Yeah," he answered happily.

After our Bible reading, we joined hands in a circle and prayed. To my surprise, God's presence was very strong. I ended the prayers and the children went outside to play. The knowledge came to me that one of the children had felt his presence so I went to the door, called them and asked if this was so. Harry answered, "Yeah, I did."

"Have you ever felt his presence like this before?"

"Oh, yes. When my little brother and I go to bed, it's a long time before I can get to sleep so I pray. It happens all the time."

It was now July and time for Eddie's party. Stuart rigged balloons on the wall of the garage and used the window as a place to rest the BB gun. We had a balloon shoot out. It was also a big success, especially with the guys!

Now the weather was warm and the neighborhood church was having Vacation Bible School, I spread the word that if anyone was interested in going; we would take them with us.

When the time came to go, we had about ten or more children gathered together in the front yard. Harry had sprained his foot and could hardly walk, but he begged his mother. Finally, she gave in. I assured her I would help him. Painfully he hobbled along. Holding hands, the children marched two by two to the church which was about four blocks away. We walked on a back street rather than the busy boulevard. Harry was struggling, we stopped and gathered around him and asked Jesus to heal him, so he could go with us and not hurt so bad. Harry ended up skipping along with no pain at all. Jesus healed Harry.

Before I would leave the house to go shopping, I always prayed and asked the Lord to help me share with someone the Good News about him. My bathroom window was small, but was bare. I felt I would like to make a curtain which I could do with just a small piece of material. One day as Robin and I went to the boulevard, as we walked down the street past the yard goods store, I felt we were supposed to go inside. I didn't have any money so I had to ignore my rationality. We entered and I looked at the small pieces of cloth. I was praying as I did this. Nothing happened so we left, saying goodbye to the owner of the store. The next day, the same thing happened. Again we left without purchasing anything, once more saying goodbye to the owner. When the following day, I felt to re-enter the same store, the owner said to me, "Well, you're getting to be as regular as the mailman." I smiled in agreement. I had some money this day, so I went to the back of the store to the small pieces of cloth and found exactly what would do nicely as an attractive window covering for my window. As I was fingering the material I heard someone say to Robin, "Little girl, do you know Jesus?" At that moment I knew this was the person I was here to meet. It's what is called, *a divine appointment*, a special meeting set up by the Lord.

She was in her late sixties or early seventies and was sitting in a chair by the counter where the owner was standing near the cash register. I went to the counter immediately, taking my cloth purchase. I replied to her question, "Yes, she does." We exchanged a few words about Jesus and she introduced herself and asked where we lived. She told me where she went to church which was nearby and invited us to come for a visit. I told her we would.

Mrs. Berger came to visit me at my home one day. She shared her testimony with me. She said she was a teacher in Russia. The educators were ordered not to share any religious information with their students especially from the Bible. She refused to obey and continued her daily routine as usual which included teaching about God. Finally after a period of time, I forget how long, she was arrested and brought before Stalin where he dealt with her. She unrelentingly held her ground. Afterward, she was taken to a cell from which the following morning, she was to be executed. During the night hours, a man came to her cell, and admonished her to quickly follow him. He opened the cell door and she did as he bade her. He led her away up into the mountains where a warm place was prepared for her. She told me she never saw his face but felt he was actually an angle sent from the Lord in her behalf. She was alone but comfortable. She told me that there was a Bible there, but it was in English and she couldn't read English. She prayed and asked the Lord to help her and he did. She then could read and understand English. Her understanding led her to be baptized later.

When we visited the church, we noticed Mrs. Berger sitting among a group which used a fourth of the pews. We learned she had visited and invited all these families to come to church. I could see the influence she made on her community. I was impressed with this Follower of Jesus.

This was also the church where I led the children in the community to the Vacation Bible School, but I never saw Mrs. Berger again.

My husband worked out of our home for a company as an appliance repairman. One evening he brought home some magazines he found discarded in a laundry room. After supper we sat at the kitchen table reading until late into the night. I was tired so I went to bed leaving him still reading at the table. As I lay in bed thinking about the testimonies I had read, I felt so close to the Lord. I felt like I could just step right into Heaven.

I looked up as something which looked like a black mist swooshed through the door into my room. As it moved it seem to stretch and then draw back into its original shape. Even though I knew it was a spirit, I had never seen anything like it before. It hovered about a foot above me and quivered. I knew it wasn't of God, and it scared me, I threw my covers over my head and thought, that's enough, no more thinking about God tonight!

The following day, forgetting about the incident the night before, I entered my prayer closet, and started praying, that same evil spirit swooshed into my closet and squirmed above me in the same threatening fashion.

Well, strong praying Christian that I was, I got out of the closet as fast as I could; Yes, closing the door behind me! Puzzled and indignant, I wondered how he could interfere if God was with me.

After a few days, I wasn't going into my closet as much as before. I "prayed as I went!" One day we learned the mother of a choir member was stricken with cancer. She was close to the choir, and we loved her. We all agreed to fast and pray for her healing.

I was fasting and praying as I had agreed, but was avoiding my closet. I had tried to pray a few more times, and the evil spirit came, so my closet was almost abandoned. When I realized this, I walked angrily with determination to *my* closet. I was taking it back! After all, we are admonished to "resist the devil, and he would flee." [34]

Sure enough, it wasn't long before the evil spirit came, and just like always, it hovered just above me, threatening me by its actions. It was at this time the Lord intervened. In a vision, I saw the closet door covered in red, and I knew it was Jesus' blood. I began to laugh deeply from within, and I knew this laughter was prompted by the Holy Spirit.

The evil spirit began to be jumbled up and weak. It was afraid, and I laughed even harder and commanded it, with great assurance, to leave my closet by the name of Jesus.

---

34 James 4:7

He swooshed immediately out of my closet. I could continue my prayer for that dear lady with faith and thanksgiving for God's mercy. He had given me back my prayer closet!

The next day with much confidence I re-entered my prayer closet as was my almost lost custom. Before long, to my astonishment, the evil spirit came back just like before.

I was puzzled and aggravated, but without fear. Once again, I stood my ground and used the authority in Jesus' name.

Out it went, and once again, I began to laugh from deep within.

The evil spirit continued to come when I prayed, but now, it was only a minor disruption. I realized that fear gives these beings power and strengthens them.

We must understand the authority we have in using Jesus' powerful name. Even spoken in conversation, it disrobes the hearers if they are in sin. The name of Jesus alone is powerful. All that we do, we do in Jesus' name. Demons recognize and hate the name of Jesus. His name has already defeated them when Jesus died on the cross. "*It is finished,*" Jesus said. We can't shoot evil spirits with a gun. We can't hit them with a bat. We can't choke them. We have to use spiritual weapons and Jesus' name is powerful. We need to study the scriptures and see the power and authority in the name of Jesus.

Are you a Believer? You shall do his deeds in Jesus' name. He is King of Kings and Lord of Lords. All power has been given unto him. Our obedience to the Holy Spirit is for Jesus' glory and the Father's glory! We are his children! [35]

---

35 Mark 16:15–20

Chapter 12

Wilderness

Stuart and I began to long for our own home away from the big city. One beautiful day; the sun was shining and the birds were singing as we visited a family in Azusa. I was ready to drop roots then and there in the foothills of the mountains.

The neighborhood was similar to what we would have liked back home in Savannah. We found a house for sale. It was shabby, but to me, it looked like my dream home, and I knew we could fix it up. Stuart and I were both anxious to make this house ours, so without delay, we contacted the real-estate company and began the process.

Not long after doing this, while in my prayer closet, I was praying when the Lord's voice, interrupted me, *"Are you willing to go through the wilderness?"*

That didn't have anything to do with what I was praying about. Thoughtfully, I replayed in my mind what I was saying before he interrupted me, but I couldn't concentrate.

Irritably, I answered, "No! Isn't that what we've already been going through? Didn't we learn the first time? You mean no job? No money? Not again!" But then, I realized, if I didn't continue to move forward, I'd go backwards. I can't stop here. I would be out of God's will. I have no choice I must go on.

Then I said, "I will if you'll go with me." I felt like crying. I knew this meant we couldn't have our new home. I thought the wilderness was: to trust God for every penny, all foods, all bills-everything. We were just getting comfortable with a job and a check on payday. I knew the Lord never failed us. We never went without our necessities, He would send it to our front door, and we never told anyone other than God of our needs. Oh, so many stories I could share, but it was hard on the flesh.

That afternoon, Stuart came home, and a man I had never met was with him. They had coffee and then the man left taking Stuart's work truck with him. My heart sank.

Stuart began to explain what was happening, but I interrupted, telling him the Lord had shown me as I was praying that morning, we would be without a job. We called the real-estate company and told them to cancel our agreement about the house but, to our astonishment and joy, they dismissed it as unimportant.

Our new house was rundown and shabby, but not without hope. We moved our furniture and few worldly possessions into our very own home. I could now stand out in my own backyard, smell the fresh air and hear the birds as they sang their sweet songs. I was home at last.

We were thrilled. Being so busy unpacking and arranging, I hadn't spent any time in my closet. In fact, these closets weren't as large as my previous one. I would have to arrange a place outside the closet to pray.

Soon, I began having headaches which was unusual for me because I was healthy. I started using aspirin for relief.

One evening, I felt lonely for the Lord. Sensing his sweetness, I rushed to the bedroom, got down on my knees and began to worship him. Immediately, a large number of black spirits swished in through the door. There were so many, they filled my room until it was black like pitch. I remained on my knees, I can't call Stuart to help me because he'll think I'm crazy! I was terrified! I had felt oppression before but never with a force actually pushing me down to the floor. Stuart can't see them! "Oh God! Oh God!" I called. There was no one to help. In this moment of being overwhelmed, I had forgotten all I had learned in the other house. I was in great distress. "Oh God! Oh God!"

All at once, I felt like I was kneeling on the top of a floor furnace. Hot wind was blowing up beneath me, and I could hear the flames of fire lapping as high as my head. Large drops of sweat were falling heavily off my body. God was present!

The multitude of black spirits swished out of the room in a frenzy, and everything subsided. Then I realized, I had subconsciously avoided praying so I wouldn't have this encounter. I wasn't so foolish this time to suppose it wouldn't happen again.

Not only did my headaches continue, but there were different manifestations occurring at various times. Evil spirits moving about at will, making noises, taking on different shapes and appearances such as huge spiders were common occurrences, especially during the night or when waking up in the morning.

My children saw these spirits also. My husband didn't see them, but showed extreme stress. Knowing I lived a clean life and loved the Lord, coupled with knowledge of the scriptures gave me security during this time. This was my home and I was indignant over the situation. I spent many nights between my two children so they could sleep. I shielded them by praying and moving my arms over each of them at the same time while the black spirits swooshed back and forth over us. I prayed as I moved my arms, and they didn't touch the children or me but I was vigilant.

I do have to add here, one night, I awoke to see a bright light reflecting off the bedroom door. I got up and crept silently over by the door, supposing someone was shining a light through the living room window. As I peeped into the living room I saw a brilliant light the height of a very tall man. I knew there were angels watching over us during this time. I didn't recall the vision of the blood of Jesus I had experienced in the closet of the previous house, but I didn't forget the Blood of Jesus.

It wasn't my house alone, but the entire neighborhood was plagued with these manifestations. When I walked down the street, I felt like I was in a pool walking in water over my head the pressure was so heavy.

A little neighborhood boy, a friend of my son, told me about this black spirit that bothered him at night. His mother told him he was having a bad dream, but he knew better. He slept with a knife to protect himself.

On a Wednesday afternoon, I decided to go and visit a new church nearby in West Covina. It was a large congregation. I sat on the left side of the center aisle half way down to the front. It was nice and comfortable, I felt at home. Toward the end of the service, the pastor opened the meeting for testimonies.

I was shaking and knew the Lord wanted me to share a dream I had the night before. In the dream my cousin Jo Ann was visiting me. I was taking her out in my backyard to show her my fruit trees that were heavy with fruit. I was proud of the beautiful, large fruit. Jo Ann said, "What are you going to do with all this fruit? If you don't pick it soon, it will fall to the ground and rot." I looked at the fruit again and realized she was right. Some of the fruit was already over ripe and needed to be picked quickly.

As I finished speaking the pastor jumped to his feet and shouted, "This is God! This is God!"

I was thankful I had shared it with the congregation but, also, I knew it had a meaning for my life personally.

The next morning I spoke with someone, and they gave me the name of an organization which ministered specifically to children. It was in a nearby town, and I called to learn more about them. The secretary answered and we began to talk. Somehow we came upon the fact of my visiting the church the night before. She also had been present and was interested in the message I shared with the congregation. She gave me a name of a person to contact who would assist in however the Lord was leading. It felt like I was feeling my way down a hall blindfolded, but I continued on in faith.

I attended a meeting of this organization and liked what I saw and heard, and sensed the Holy Spirit drawing me to begin this work. I didn't have the finances to do all I wanted, but these two ladies offered to assist me in getting started. One lady did my flannel for scenes for the Life of Christ figures. I went to a Christian Book Store and bought the *Life of Christ Book* which gave me the figures and directions on how and when to use them. Stuart made me a flannel board. I also bought two or three visual songs and the ladies showed me how to make others. Now I was ready to do this work in the neighborhood.

One early morning, Robin was standing on the table as I hemmed her dress. Jenny, a young neighbor was watching. I don't remember exactly what was being said, but it must have been about Jesus because she said, "I want to go to church with you and get Jesus in my heart."

No one had ever been so direct with me before, and it surprised me. "You don't have to go to church to have Jesus come in your heart. We can pray right here and now and he'll do that for you."

"He will?"

"Yes. Do you want to give Jesus your heart now?"

I helped Robin down from the table. "Come on Jenny, let's go in Robin's room and pray," I said leading her down the hall.

We got down on our knees beside the bed. I prayed first then led Jenny in a prayer of repentance and dedication. When we finished praying, she was full of joy.

The next day Jenny returned with Becky, her middle sister. Jenny was the youngest of three girls.

"Becky wants Jesus to come into her heart too," she said.

"Becky, would you like to ask Jesus to come into your heart right now?" I asked.

She smiled shyly, "Yes Ma'am."

The three of us went into Robin's room to pray. Like Jenny, she received the joy and peace Jesus gives to those who come to him. The Holy Spirit witnessed with their spirits that they were truly God's children. The Spirit himself testifies with our spirit that we are God's children." [36]

I wondered what their parents would think about all of this since these girls were so happy with Jesus. I knew they wouldn't keep it to themselves and their new dispositions would cause the parents to question them.

Their mother was often in deep depression and radiated unhappiness. She worked hard to discipline and to teach the girls responsibility. I could tell she really loved them, and took her responsibility as a mother seriously. They did their chores, and stayed close to home. However, she had a problem; she was addicted to alcohol and gambling. Their father was a former member of the Mafia. I knew Jesus would enter that home, and bring a challenge to both parents.

---

36 Romans 8:16

It wasn't long after this time when Jenny told me her mom had opened the telephone book and randomly called a minister of a Methodist church from a nearby town. She invited him over to talk about this which was happening with her girls.

I knew many in the religious community hadn't experienced and didn't understand the new birth, and I was concerned. I didn't want anything negative to touch what the Lord had begun in this family. In prayer I asked the Lord, "If this minister isn't one of yours, don't let him keep this appointment. If he is yours, please witness with his spirit what you are doing."

Nervously, I kept a close eye on their house. I felt like a mother bird with a crow flying nearby, eyeing her young ones. Finally, the minister arrived and went inside their house. I went into prayer. Later Jenny and Becky came over. They liked the minister. After they shared with him what they had to say, he affirmed this was indeed God for their lives. He invited the whole family to attend his church, which they did. "Praise the Lord!"

At this time, Linda, the teen-age daughter, did not come to my house, but God continued to work in this home.

Chapter 13

God in the Wilderness

A boy named Terry was sweet on Linda, and it wasn't a secret. I don't know how she felt about him, but her parents kept a close eye on their girls, especially Linda, who was a pretty blond with a bubbly disposition.

I was told Terry, who was fourteen years old and his Dad beat up two policemen just the week before. His dad was addicted to alcohol and his mother had recently left home. They didn't know where she was. Terry had two young siblings; one was a pre-school age, the other a baby. It was a heavy responsibility on such a young boy to care for the young children. His dad would see there was food in the house before he began drinking on the weekend. This was another hurting family in great need of the Lord.

It was getting dark, time for Eddie and Robin to come in and have supper, so I went to my kitchen window and called them. There were teen-agers in the street hanging out and when they heard me call, they came to my window. I knew all of them except for a boy sitting on a bicycle.

Linda said, "Mrs. Osland, my aunt came to see us the other day. She's a nun, but she doesn't talk about Jesus like you do."

"Well Linda, maybe she doesn't know him like I do."

Quickly, Terry interjected, "Yeah, but you know when you read the *Bible,* and it's pretty hard to believe some of that stuff!"

"Yes, you're right, but just let the Holy Spirit touch you one time, and then you'll know God can do anything!"

Suddenly, Terry was pushed into the wall of my house next to my window!

Astonished I said, "Do you know what that was?"

The new boy on the bicycle said, "That was the Holy Spirit!"

"Yes, it was, I said!"

Terry was the oldest of the group and held the title, of the Neighborhood Bully. He began to cry openly, even in front of the girl he cared so much about.

Realizing this was a *God moment* for these children, I told them, "I was twenty-five years old before I got saved. It's not a thing to be ashamed of because Jesus said you can't see the Kingdom of Heaven unless you are born again. He didn't say it was a good idea, or that you should consider it, or that it was an option. "*Jesus said, 'you must be born again!*' "

"Since I was a lot older than you are now when I was born again, I won't make fun of you. If you want to be born again, just knock on my door and tell me. I'll pray with you."

At this point I was shaking, and again I called my children as the teen-agers began to wander back out into the street. I shut my window. I was hardly able to comprehend what had just happened.

I knew this was an extraordinary visitation from the Lord so when putting supper on the table, I asked the Lord, "Please don't let Terry forget what happened."

I later heard he had come down with the measles and was confined to his house. I wasn't worried about his health but smiled remembering my prayer. A couple of weeks passed and I heard knocking on my front door. When I opened it, there stood Terry and Brad, the boy who lived across the street with his step-mother.

Terry stammered, "Mrs. Osland, now what did you say we had to do to be born again?"

I invited them to come in and explained, just like I had to Jenny. They said this was definitely what they wanted so I led them into my son's room where we got on our knees. I prayed first and then led them in a prayer of repentance and dedication. The presence of the Lord was tremendous, and they just ended their prayer laughing. The Holy Spirit had done what the *Bible* tells us he would do. He witnessed with each one, they were truly God's children. All convictions of sin were gone, all things were brand new. They had peace, joy and also rest for their souls regardless of their outward circumstances, just like it is written in the *Bible*. "The Spirit itself beareth witness with our spirit, that we are the children of God." [37]

The family who lived next door to me was Roman Catholic and very good neighbors. Robin played with their youngest son who was four-year-old. They also had two teen-age sons and an older teen-age daughter.

One day the youngest teen-age son, Richard, knocked on my door.

"Hi," I said.

"Hello, Mrs. Osland," he replied.

He was a well-adjusted young man who knew how to talk to adults; he wasn't shy and without hesitation, he began, "Mrs. Osland, I've been trying to get Terry to go to my church with me. He always gave me a hard time, threatening and bullying me. I believed if he would start going to church, he would stop treating me that way. He came close to going, but never did. I've seen a difference in the way he acts. He doesn't bully me anymore, and I just want to know what church he's going to?"

"Well, Richard, he goes with us, but that wasn't what made the difference in his life."

"What did?"

"He gave his heart to Jesus and was born again."

"Oh, what's that?"

"Do you have a *Bible*?"

"Yes."

"Go get it and I'll show you." We opened his *Bible* to John, chapter 3. Verse 1:

"There was a man of the Pharisees, named Nicodemus, a ruler of the Jews: The same came to Jesus by night, and said unto him, 'Rabbi, we know that thou art a teacher come from God: for no man can do these miracles that thou doest, except God be with him.' "

"Jesus answered and said unto him, 'Verily, verily, I say unto thee, except a man be born again, he cannot see the kingdom of God.' "

"Nicodemus saith unto him, 'how can a man be born when he is old? Can he enter the second time into his mother's womb, and be born?' "

---

37 Romans 8:16

"*Jesus answered, 'Verily, verily, I say unto thee, except a man be born of water and of the Spirit, he cannot enter into the kingdom of God. That which is born of the flesh is flesh; and that which is born of the Spirit is spirit. Marvel not that I said unto thee, Ye must be born again.*

The wind bloweth where it listeth (chooses), and thou hearest the sound thereof, but canst not tell whence it cometh, and whither it goeth: so is every one that is born of the Spirit.'"

"*Nicodemus answered and said unto him, 'how can these things be?'*

"*Jesus answered and said unto him, 'Art thou a master of Israel, and knowest not these things?' "38*

After reading the scripture, I said, "Richard did you see where Jesus said, 'You *must* be born again?' " It's necessary in order to enter the kingdom of Heaven. You know Nicodemus was not only a good man, but he was a religious leader who taught others. If anyone should have known this, he should have."

Richard, now excited said, "Mrs. Osland. I'm born again!"

I was taken aback by his declaration, so doubtfully I asked, "Tell me about it. When did it happen, and where?"

He seemed very solemn as he began his story. "In my church the time had come for me to be made a Soldier of the Cross. I had done everything required except one thing. I was supposed to go to the priest to confess my sins, and I did except for one thing. I was so ashamed and I couldn't tell him about it. I was so troubled; I went to the altar and confessed to the Lord. I cried and cried but I still couldn't go to the priest. However, as I prayed at the altar, something happened to me from God. I got up knowing my sin had been forgiven, and I felt different, like I had never felt before. I know I was born again at that time."

I was elated to hear his testimony, and the Holy Spirit blessed us as we finished our time together. "Richard, you need to study your *Bible* so you can encourage others and grow into a strong Christian man."

Several days later, he told me his family was unhappy about him reading the *Bible*, but he was going to continue anyway.

As I was going to the doors of my neighborhood, I approached a home diagonally across from mine. I didn't see this family very often but knew there were about five children. They invited me in while I explained about the children's *Bible* club which would be held in my

---

38 John 3:1–10

home. They agreed to let their children attend. The wife shared with me that they had been having a hard time. Her husband had been out of work for awhile and couldn't seem to find a job. I believe there had been illness also. As I left, I sympathized with their situation. I said I would be praying for them. On my way to the next house, my heart was touched for this family knowing how many children were involved and was probably doing without their necessities. This scripture began to trouble me: "What doth it profit, my brethren, though a man say he hath faith, and have not works? Can faith save him? If a brother or sister be naked, and destitute of daily food, and one of you say unto them, 'Depart in peace, be ye warmed and filled'; notwithstanding ye give them not those things which are needful to the body; what doth it profit?' Even so faith, if it hath not works, is dead, being alone."[39]

I was ignorant of the suffering this family was going through, but the Lord wasn't.

When I came home at the end of the day, happy about all the homes I had visited, meeting neighbors for the first time, yet I was still troubled about the family nearby. I went into my bedroom and sat down at the desk. I pulled out our household ledger and opened it to the back page. There were several weeks of money set aside to give to the Lord. I was holding it until we had settled in at a new church. I couldn't hold this money knowing what the Bible said. I spoke with my husband, and he agreed we should give it to this family in Jesus' name.

I immediately sat down, wrote a short note and sent it to them with the money.

A few days later one of their children handed me a note saying: "Thank you for all you have done. My father is a Baptist minister, and we knew the right way." The note said also they knew it was God, and they called a nearby church and made an appointment to meet with the pastor in his office. While with him, they gave their lives to Jesus, and were going to attend that church. She said her husband used the money to join a union which provided him with the much needed job.

The same day I met this family, I also met a lady, Mrs. Newsome. When I knocked on her door, she answered, and as I told her who I was, and what I was doing, she was very receptive. She didn't invite me

---

39 James 2:14–17

in, and I noticed she still had on her bathrobe, and it was afternoon. Moreover, she seemed to be holding tightly to the door.

"My dear, I'm a Christian, and I love the Lord, but I've been very sick."

"Then I'm certain you know about the gifts of healing given by the Holy Spirit," I said.

"Yes, I believe Jesus heals today."

"I have a Christian friend that lives nearby. If you like, we'll seek the Lord and come back to pray for your healing. I'll call and let you know when."

She was so appreciative and my heart was moved, seeing she was alone and ill.

I called my friend Doris, who lived down the street from me, and asked if she would go and pray for Mrs. Newsome with me. She reluctantly agreed which puzzled me. She was so enthusiastic when praying for people when at church. I knew she struggled with her health, but I also thought perhaps she might receive healing also.

When the day came, we went to Mrs. Newsome's house. She greeted us and we all went into her den. After a few minutes of becoming better acquainted, we got on our knees to seek the Lord. Then Doris and I got up and walked toward Mrs. Newsome who was now standing, and before we could reach her, she kicked off her shoes and fell backwards on the floor. We stood a few feet away and worshipped the Lord. As she lay there she began telling us what was happening to her. The presence of the Lord was powerful in that room.

She said, "The Lord spoke and told me to take off my shoes because I was on holy ground, and it feels like warm oil is flowing down my esophagus into my stomach." After a few seconds she said, "I feel my kidney moving up in place." She continued giving us the details which I cannot remember.

When we left Mrs. Newsome's house, we were full of joy and victory. We had been in God's presence and viewed a miracle. How blessed we were (especially Mrs. Newsome!), but Doris kept saying, "The Lord told her to remove her shoes for she was on holy ground. Do you know what that makes us?"

I ignored her and didn't answer which was wrong of me. I should have withstood her that very moment. The *holy ground* Mrs. Newsome was standing upon was because of God's presence, not ours. He was answering many of his children's prayers when He healed her. [40]

The following day, I was at the school bus stop waiting for Robin to come home from kindergarten when Mrs. Newsome walked up to me. We greeted each other with a big hug, and laughter.

She told me that right after we left her house, she could scrub her kitchen floor on her hands and knees. Again, we just laughed and praised the Lord. She then said, she was a Sunday school teacher of young married couples at a Four-Square church. She said her class was outgrowing all the other classes, and they had to split it up. God was using her greatly until she got sick with leukemia. She was in the late stage of this disease along with other ailments. She said God had completely healed and restored her.

I was shocked. I assumed she perhaps had the flu with other minor complications. I was so happy I hadn't asked details because, oh, my little faith!

She told me my friend had come right back to her house, asking her to write out her testimony, so she could put it in her book. It was evident that Doris wanted to take the credit for the miracle. Mrs. Newsome recognized this as Doris' ego, and being a mature Christian, she would not comply with her request.

That Doris had returned so quickly to her house surprised me, and I was disappointed she had attempted to take credit for what God had done. I knew something was wrong but hadn't faced the problem with Doris. I guess I was deliberately avoiding the confrontation. My husband saw the problem and so did Doris' husband, in fact, they even discussed it. I fussed and defended her which didn't help her at all. I was closing my eyes.

---

40 Exodus 3:5–6

Chapter 14

Victory in the Wilderness

The teen-age girls assisted me with the Bible club, and they led the singing using large posters printed with words and illustrations of the songs. They also taught memory verses printed on multi-colored construction paper.

We would separate the words and glue a small piece of flannel to the back of each individual word which caused them to stick to the flannel on the board. Then as the group read the entire memory verse a couple of times, we would call on a child to come and remove a word. Then they would read out loud in unison the verse filling in the blank space by memory. We would do this repeatedly until all of the words had been removed and the board was empty. Whoever could remember the missing words would stand and recite the entire verse. The children loved reading and reciting the memory verses and were always eager to participate. Then it was time for the Bible story. I told the story placing the flannel figures in the scenes colored with pastels. There were desert, town, mountain, manger and other scenes needed for The Life of Christ. Afterwards the girls served cookies and Kool-Aid. In a three month period approximately 135 children accepted Jesus as their Savior.

Returning home from a weekend trip, we were driving slowly down our street when we saw Terry, Brad and another boy pushing their bikes. They motioned for us to stop the car, and we rolled down the window. They pointed to the other boy with them and said, "He wants to be born again, too!" God had begun a work on the street among the teens, especially the boys.

We had been living in our house for almost a year. By reason of the continuing demonic conflict (headaches, pains on my body, lack of sleep, and demons openly showing themselves) since moving into this house, I was tired. During this year I had approached many pastors, evangelists and leaders explaining our plight. I was weary of having to profess my clean life, so they would know I wasn't inviting these demonic presences by an impure lifestyle. By reason of their lack of knowledge and experience in spiritual warfare, I received many different responses. They always made me feel as though I was dirty. These people I believed were of authority in the Bible, having been to the seminaries and Bible colleges. Since we couldn't find anyone to help, I lost hope and accepted the fact we were living in these conditions and didn't know when we would ever get out.

Once I settled the thought of never getting help or ever getting out, as tired as I was, I felt I was supposed to fast, drinking only water, for seven days. I had fasted short times, but never for so long. The scriptures instruct us how we should fast.

Jesus tells us we should fast *secretly* even taking care in our personal grooming so no one can tell we are fasting. [41]

However, the scripture on my heart told of a man who brought his son, who was tormented by a demon, to the disciples, and they couldn't deliver him. When Jesus arrived, the father told him about the situation. Jesus cast the demon out of the son. When the disciples asked why they could not cast him out, He told them it was due to their unbelief. "Moreover, He said, this one could not be cast out without fasting and prayer." [42]

I told my husband what I felt I should do, and he was supportive. My house was neglected by the time the fast was ending. He understood and never complained. I have a wonderful husband. If you had asked me why I fasted, I would only say, "obedience."

The next Sunday as the congregation finished praying at the church altar, I was returning to my seat when Doris came up to me and asked,

---

41 Matthew 6:16–18
42 Matthew 17:14–21.

"What are you asking God for, while you are fasting?" I was surprised. I didn't know how she knew what I was doing.

I said, "Nothing!" and continued walking, hoping she would get the message.

Instead, following me she persisted, "Girl, you can ask for anything and get it. Why are you not asking for things?"

I didn't answer her.

This upset me because she was intruding where she didn't belong.

I was happy when the seven days were finished. I'll admit my stupidity in ending the fast at a buffet.

There seemed to be a change for the better. One outstanding change, we were re-united with our dear friends, Lucy, Jay and Ronnie, we loved so much.

They later shared why the division in our fellowship. Someone visited them with a doctrine that wasn't correct, and influenced them against us. They later realized what had happened. Meanwhile we had moved and they couldn't locate us. They met up with Doris and she mentioned us and where we were living. That's how they came to see us one evening.

Stuart was at work. I fixed coffee and we sat in the kitchenette while their teen-age son sat in the living room. As we talked, I took a deep breath and began telling them about "the house."

Jay stopped me, "Now, Tommie." He started to stroke his mustache and chuckle.

When he did this, I knew I was in trouble and waited for his lecture. Irritated, I thought, Jay knows the way I live. I don't invite this kind of presence.

"Demons don't want to live in your house. They want to live in your body!" He said in a gentle, yet serious way, looking intensely into my eyes making sure I understood what he was saying.

Frustrated, here we go again, my friends! I almost couldn't control the emotions I was experiencing. Shakily, I replied, "I know! But, they can't!"

Suddenly, Ronnie cried out in the living room. We jumped up and ran to him. When we reached him, he was choking.

We prayed.

He was holding his throat and crying hard, "They choked me!"

Jay asked me what I had done about this situation.

I told him about contacting all the pastors and evangelists who hadn't been able to help. Then I mentioned calling the nearest Assembly of God church. I spoke with the pastor and told him the story and asked for his help. He told me he wasn't familiar with situations of this sort, but there was an elderly missionary couple in his church who could possibly help me. He gave me Mr. and Mrs. Cannon's telephone number. When I hung up I just put the number away."

Jay said emphatically, "Call that number, *now!*"

I called and when Mrs. Cannon answered, I told her the pastor had given me their number thinking perhaps they could help us. I further explained about my house and the experience we had just had. To my utter amazement, she understood everything I told her. This was the first time anyone had understood. Even my husband had thought I was off center here.

She said, "Join hands and pray, plead the Blood of Jesus over you, resisting the evil one before you come to our home. We'll be expecting you shortly."

We joined hands and prayed as they had instructed us. Then I got my children out of bed, dressed them and went with Jay, Lucy and Ronnie to the home of the missionaries.

Again we shared what happened to Ronnie. I explained everything I could remember my family and I had gone through the previous year. None of this was strange to them. They knew exactly what I was talking about.

At last!

The Cannons shared some experiences they had as missionaries. They went to the Virgin Islands without any knowledge of spiritual warfare. While the Cannons were going through orientation, one of the missionaries already stationed there tried to share with them, but was silenced by the other missionaries.

Even today, the churches remain silent on these issues while the world offers answers and entertainment to our children in these areas. This silence withholds important information necessary to resist our spiritual enemy as you probably can already see from my story.

It wasn't long before the Cannons learned firsthand about spiritual warfare from personal experiences they encountered. They shared some of their life story with us. They held the key to my dilemma and told us that they and some friends would come and "pray through my house."

It sounded strange like superstition, but all of this was strange. I had never in all my life heard about things I was experiencing. But I was anxious for this to be over, if they had told me to go home and stand on my head in a corner for two hours, believe me, I would have struggled to do it.

My concern was, will Stuart still be at work? I didn't want him to fuss. I told them the best time to come would be late in the afternoon while he would be working.

I was determined to do what the missionaries told me. They gave examples and stories from the mission field. Before I was saved I never believed in spiritual happenings, and I thought they were magic tricks to fool people. I could laugh at children's magicians, (my uncle was one), but I had little tolerance for adult performances especially in religious situations, to which I attributed the few healings I had ever seen. At the time, I wasn't born again so I was ignorant of what the Bible taught.

The Cannons instructed me to dispose of all material which had been given to me by Doris so I went home and did what they said. I went to Doris' to give her the curtains and a few odds and ends she gave me when we moved in, but she didn't answer the door. I placed the box where she would see it. We hadn't yet spoken, but I was determined to break our fellowship that day. I wanted everything to be in order when the Cannon's and their friends came to pray through my house. When they came everything was ready for their ministry.

When it was late afternoon, Jay, Lucy and Ronnie arrived. Then the pastor of the church came, but didn't stay. Then Mr. and Mrs. Cannon and their friends arrived. As we all were in my living room, Mrs. Cannon saw an evil spirit go through the room, but no one else saw it.

We followed the group as they got up and went to the back room which was Eddie's bedroom. They began praying and moving about the room. I got close so I could hear exactly what they were saying. If this happened to me again, I would know what to do.

Prayerfully we left the bedroom and moved to the next room. As we were approaching the bedroom nearest the living room, my daughter's bedroom, Stuart came home. My heart almost jumped out of my body, but I thought never mind, don't stop! A matter of seconds passed, no one hesitated in their praying. There was a loud cry from Ronnie and at the same moment, we heard Stuart exclaim. At that point, no one paused, we were still praying, but I was listening and also wondering what had happened in the living room.

We finally finished praying through the house, and everyone was introduced to Stuart when Ronnie excitedly told us what he had seen. He and Stuart both saw the same thing at the same time. It was a manifestation of a wrinkled, old man who was bent over, knees high near his chest, jumping through the living room then going into my daughter's bedroom.

Whew, I thought, now I don't have to explain to Stuart what was happening. I was greatly relieved. We said our goodbyes and everyone left. I could hardly believe it was over. No more troubled, sleepless nights. It was finished and we could now live a normal life. It was late. We were exhausted and went to bed.

During the night I could hear Eddie moving about in his bed and knew he was restless. I got up and went to his bed to lie down with him. As I was going back to sleep, I saw a black spirit swish over us, and then it swished back over us. Each time when he swished over, we would turn over.

I said out loud, "By faith you aren't here!" That didn't work! It kept moving back and forth.

Then I realized I had to say the words to the evil spirit the missionaries used in their prayers.

I said, "I plead the blood of Jesus against you. I bind you in the name of Jesus and command you to leave this room, this house and this property and go into the deep to await judgment. I pray this in the Name of Jesus Christ." [43]

When I spoke to him in the name and authority of Jesus and commanded him to leave, he went out of Eddie's window. The rest of the night was peaceful. Indeed, this was the effective weapon to use to overcome evil spirits.

What a difference it was living in our house after they had prayed. I felt like pulling the curtains closed and letting the world go by. I knew

---

43 Please see Afterword for details and scripture which would support and explain the missionary's prayer.

I couldn't do it and rejected my selfish desires. However, my house remained restful in spite of all the ongoing traffic.

Our one main disturbance remaining was Robin's poor health. She was experiencing bouts of severe pain in her stomach. She would be in agony crying for her daddy. I would call Stuart at work, but by the time he could get home, she would be completely normal. The doctor did many tests but they revealed nothing.

She was five years old and during a visit to his office, I was sitting in the examining room while the doctor and nurse were working with her. Joking, she said to them, "I'm just a hypochondriac!" The doctor and nurse turned and looked accusingly at me.

Oh, how I would have liked to have gotten hold of him at that moment! I explained Stuart teased her saying this. I don't know if they believed me or not, but we had been seeing this doctor for a long time. I hoped he had more confidence in me.

Sadly, we were nearing the end of knowing what to do for her when the doctor told me there was only one last test he could do. He could test her for an ulcer, but he didn't believe she had this problem due to her age. When the results came back it revealed a duodenal ulcer. Everyone was surprised and I was thankful they had found the source of her pain.

Early into treatment, the Lord healed Robin. One day, Mrs. Cannon told me while praying for her; she had a witness from the Lord that Robin was healed. We relaxed the treatment and broadened her variety of foods. When they tested her again, the x-ray showed it was gone.

One morning early, I was working in my back yard; I greatly disliked the bush under Eddie's window which was my favorite flower. It was a large red geranium bush rather than a potted plant, like we have in Georgia. I decided to break the bush into pieces and root them. I thought it would be beautiful as a red floral hedgerow.

As I was digging under the bush, to my surprise, I found a fetish which is an object used in witchcraft. I questioned one of my neighbors who told me witchcraft had been practiced over the family living in the house before us!

The Cannon's told me, this was important, because it was the object they cursed to be used for the house, I supposed like a point of contact. My dislike for the bush, which puzzled me since that was my favorite flower, gave me the desire to remove it, otherwise, I would have never found it. Thus, I discovered the evil object used in performing the witchcraft.

I could easily see how our wonderful Lord moved the mountains of despair after I fasted before him. Everything is in his timing, and we always learn lessons to make us useful for his kingdom.

Chapter 15

The Seducer Revealed

The seducing spirit is so important this day in the religious world. He is actively trying to pass as the Holy Spirit and is successful with many. I have endeavored to write about him many times, but have experienced spiritual opposition, and I succumbed rather than persevered. Bear with me as I refer back to when I first met Doris. [44]

When my husband and I were members of a large choir at a church in Los Angeles, the altar calls, with its prayer ministries, were large. I watched an attractive lady, in a green dress, with upswept light red hair, move from one prayer group to another. She had an air of authority, and I wondered who she was.

Lucy and Jay met Doris first and introduced us. Her husband, Thomas, never came forward until after the prayer time was finished. He was quiet and very likeable where she was bubbly and praised the Lord a lot and drew much attention.

One night Doris and Thomas invited me, Stuart, and the children over to their house for a meal and fellowship. Thomas was a car salesman and dressed well. Although quiet, he was pleasant and mild mannered and seemed to walk in Doris' shadow. While we were there, we enjoyed our visit. In fact, their house was just down the street from the house

---

44 2 Corinthians 11:13–15

we would soon buy. I was thrilled at the thought of having such an exuberant Christian living nearby.

I did visit with Doris, and she with me, but not very often, because though I enjoyed having good neighbors, my days were filled with caring for my home, study and prayer. She stayed in her home most of the time, and I never recall seeing her outside in the neighborhood. Although she had a well-manicured yard, I don't believe she spent much time there.

During my time with her, I began to detect something was not right, but couldn't put my finger on it. She talked often about how different people bragged about her having "old time power" when she prayed, and I could tell flattery was crucial to her. She was very different in her daily living than when in church. Most of the time at home; she was solemn, almost gloomy, yet in church, she was so exuberant, she stood out among the people. That's why I noticed her at the church meeting. I didn't know how long she had lived in this location, but she told me how the neighborhood children made fun of her because she prayed. She said she rebuked them once and God knocked them to the ground. I was uneasy as she told me that.

We didn't share in the scriptures very much. In fact, when we were together with Jay and Lucy reading the Bible, she told me privately pertaining to Jay, reading the scriptures was a distraction of the devil to keep us from prayer.

She told me of a disagreement she had with her sister, and said, "Something just took my hand and brought it down hitting her!" As she was talking, she made a fist, and mimed hitting someone. I was not only shocked, but angry. "Doris! Don't you dare tell me the Holy Spirit took your hand and hit your sister?" This was the only time I ever withstood her.

She sputtered and didn't have an answer, but then she tried to reinforce what she had intimated.

I thought. That does it! I'm through. I didn't tell Stuart about her saying this.

One afternoon, Thomas came over alone, which was unusual, for a cup of coffee and to talk. Even though I was working in another part of the house, I could hear some of what he was saying. She called him one day at work to tell him she had seen a vision of him driving home on the interstate when his car caught on fire, and he was killed. Thomas was frightened because many things she saw came to pass.

I understood his fear, because even though she carried a Bible and named the name of Jesus, her behavior caused me to be confused. At my young Christian age, knowing the scriptures, I couldn't comprehend God filling someone with such power when their lives didn't have the fruits of the Holy Spirit such as, love, joy, peace, and holiness reflecting and glorifying Christ.

Thomas said other things after I returned to the kitchen, and I became very nervous that her husband was talking about her. I realized then, I didn't want to believe anything negative about her, or have a confrontation, even though I could see there were problems.

He told us Doris was from a poor family. He also said, she never got the attention or love, she needed. After she got saved, she went to "work" in a prayer room in a huge, famous church downtown. She often boasted they would say, "Yes Ma'am, you've got that old timey power when you pray!" They began to admire, elevate her, and she felt important. She began to take a leading role and even tried to control the prayer room. Thomas said eventually there was a disagreement, and they rejected her, causing emotional injury, and now, she was almost a recluse except when she felt like going to a church. They weren't members of any particular church, so they didn't go very often.

He then spoke to me, "She sleeps all day and stays awake all night. I need help. Tommie, will you call and get her to do something, so she'll stay out of bed?"

In my heart I didn't want to commit myself, but I was troubled for her, so I agreed. The next day I tried to get her to go to the grocery store with me, but she declined. She wasn't interested in going anywhere or doing anything. I felt sorry for Thomas, but I couldn't help him.

Doris knew, at times, I could see evil spirits when they were present and one day, she said, "Only demon-possessed people can see evil spirits." It felt like she had slapped my face, but I didn't oppose her statement.

A few days later when Stuart, I and the children were on the freeway going home, we all were quiet. I was thinking about what Doris had said, and out loud, I said, "*I don't believe that!*" As I refuted what she had said, to my surprise, something spiritual left my presence.

Spoken words can be conduits of faith or fear. Words are powerful and can influence the hearers in a negative or positive way. Words can be energized by spirits influencing unsuspecting people. This is why some things spoken to us have more impact than the same words spoken at other times by different people. The scripture says:

"But I say unto you, that every idle word that men shall speak, they shall give account thereof in the Day of Judgment. For by thy words thou shalt be justified, and by thy words thou shalt be condemned."[45]

Whenever she did read or share the scriptures, Doris' interpretation was always confusing. She never considered the scripture's context, and I couldn't understand how she came to her conclusions.

Jay was a licensed and ordained minister and Thomas asked him if he would counsel them about their marriage, and he agreed. Jay asked me to continue my relationship with Doris until after he could meet and counsel them. Hesitantly, I agreed. Jay and Lucy had always been such good friends of ours. Our relationship seemed to cause friction within Doris, and she began acting hostile toward me especially when Jay and Lucy were present.

When the children's Bible clubs began, Doris was energized to the point of wanting to take a leading role, but I wouldn't let her come due to her instability. I told the parents of these children I would teach from the Bible without any influence from any denomination. Also, I encouraged the families to attend the churches of their choice because most didn't attend church of any denomination. If they asked my guidance, I would suggest a church I knew that presented the Gospel. She accepted my reasoning peacefully but with disdain.

From reading the Bible and also, the testimonies of Christians from the Classics, I understood the power of the Holy Spirit filled, consecrated people of God. In the lives where the Holy Spirit's power was observed, the fruits were also evident. This puzzled me because this didn't describe Doris. Where did the power she possessed come from? Perhaps a better phrased question would be: *What power possessed Doris?*

One evening Doris prayed for Jay. I was standing beside him when this force picked him up off his feet, turning him around in the air

---

45 Matthew 12:36–37

until he almost hit the ceiling. I laughed, but as he got up off the floor, he looked sternly at me and said, "That wasn't the Holy Ghost!"

"What was it?" I asked.

"I don't know, but I'm going to find out."

At this time, we were young in the faith, but knowledgeable in the scriptures. We were learning about the great power of the Holy Spirit in the lives of the apostles from the book of Acts. We were impressed by the stories and desired this same power for our lives as witnesses for Jesus. What we were experiencing with Doris conflicted with what we knew.

Jay came to my house a few days later and before greeting me, he said, "It was the seducing spirit!" I knew he was referring to what happened at Doris' house.

At this time, we joined hands and prayed for them and us. Jay told us that the Lord revealed to him, Doris would lose her mind, which saddened all of us.

When something spiritual happens, often people automatically attribute it to God not realizing *Satan is a spiritual entity*. This is chilling, but a fact which we must acknowledge. He is actively moving and working as deception in this day. If he is tolerated, he will slowly work his way into our lives until he finds a weakness where he can manifest himself. At this time, I recognized evil spirits. They usually were black and in the shape of what you would think a spirit would look like. I could also discern their presence. Where seducing spirits are also evil, they are more difficult to discern. At this time, I wasn't aware of seducing spirits and as far as I knew, I hadn't yet seen one. The reaction to evil spirits usually is repulsion, where the seducing spirit attracts and draws. There is a resemblance of peace which eventually robs your vitality and neutralizes your interest in the things of God. You become very tired physically and spiritually, like one suffering from iron deficiency. Your mind becomes sluggish, making it difficult to think clearly. This was the second thing I was to learn from being in the wilderness.

Mr. and Mrs. Cannon, the missionaries, advised me immediately, to remove any articles Doris had given me from my home. I didn't understand what the condition of my house had to do with Doris.

Nevertheless, I did this to prepare for the upcoming day they were going to pray through my home.

After eliminating the few things I had (leaving them in a box near her door when she didn't answer the door), I never spoke with her again. She already had strong feelings against me and began telling people I was calling her a witch. I never associated her with such a title.

Leslie, a mutual friend, asked me, "What is wrong with Doris? When I go to see her, I feel fine, but when I leave, I have hate in my heart. What's wrong?"

I hadn't told her anything. I hadn't said anything to anyone. So, as kindly as I could, I explained everything I knew. After that day, she and her children were buying groceries in a large store, when Doris saw her. In a loud, projected voice, she began to "prophesy!" Leslie hurried the children out of the store.

Leslie's husband, Carrol, wanted to attend a big meeting with a well known evangelist. She didn't want to go, being familiar with Doris' situation. We all were trying to avoid anything unfamiliar by this time. Jay, Lucy, Stuart and I agreed to go with them, so they wouldn't be alone. We joined hands in prayer asking God's covering. We went as observers, not worshippers.

During the service, the evangelist called out a lady from the audience, and told the audience, "This lady has a severe breaking out all over her back."

Her response was, "I do?"

The lady just happened to be Doris. Since it was on her back, he could not show her malady to the onlookers. They continued to perform, Doris agreeing with him.

This was the last time I saw her, but I received hateful telephone calls from people I didn't even know accusing me of my wrongful treatment of Doris. When I tried to reason with them, they would hang up.

My next door neighbor's (the one whose son told me he was born again) sister lived next door to Doris. She called me on the phone and said, "I know you and Doris go to the same church, and I felt I needed to call and tell you what's happened. This morning as my sister was cleaning her pool, Doris came to the fence, called out in a loud voice saying, "The Lord's told me to kill you!" She paused–

"I'm so sorry this has happened, but Doris and I don't attend the same church. I guess you haven't noticed, but we haven't seen each other in awhile. I believe you should tell your sister, if Doris said this, she means it. She and her family should be extremely careful and take precautions."

The Lord was blessing the children's Bible Clubs. They were flourishing, and the children were hungry to hear the stories from the Bible. I was eager to share; many were receiving Christ as their personal Savior.

The pressure from the evil spirits in our home was heavy. We weren't sleeping well. One night I awoke and saw the silhouette of a tall man standing by my bed. I couldn't see his features because he was full of and surrounded by brilliant light. There was peace and I knew it was one of the Lord's angels. Experiences like this happened sporadically which reinforced my faith and sense of security.

Stuart was away many hours during the day because we owned a Laundromat which he had to clean after he finished his regular job. When he got home, the tension was great. He couldn't see the activity of these spirits but with little sleep, it was stressful. His eyes were bloodshot and he was miserable.

When in prayer one morning I sensed he was going to suffer. My imagination began to run so I called Lucy. I told her how I felt and asked for their prayers. I was afraid for him.

That afternoon when Stuart came home, he felt like he was catching a cold. It was payday, so we decided to go out for supper. We went to a Mexican buffet, and I looked for the Chili Relleno, but I didn't see it. I assumed it wasn't on the buffet. When I went to the table, I saw perspiration rolling down Stuart's face. I asked him what he was eating. It was the dish I wanted. I decided I really didn't want it if it was that hot.

I awoke about two in the morning and Stuart was sitting on the side of the bed, bent over holding his stomach, groaning. A few weeks after we first arrived in Los Angeles, he was taken to the emergency room with the same kind of pain. They said he had pleurisy and to put hot, moist towels on him, so I treated him the same at this time. I kept increasing the heat until it was almost burning my hands. Nothing helped.

When daylight came, I called Jay and asked if they would come and take us to the emergency room. They were dressed for church when they arrived and after Stuart was admitted into the hospital, he was given strong medication but his pain was still intense. The doctor he needed to see wouldn't be available until the next day.

When we left the hospital, Jay and Lucy wanted to go to church. I had been up all night and wasn't dressed for church. I even had on my bedroom slippers. Then I thought what better place to be at this time than with God's people?

When we started to sing, I felt the Lord's presence and just melted into tears which had been pent up in my concern for Stuart. When your spouse hurts, you hurt. Suddenly, my tears were replaced with laughter from deep within. God was in control, I needn't worry. My anxiety had been replaced with peace.

When the doctor tested Stuart, they revealed his gallbladder needed to be removed. At that time, it was a very serious operation. In fact, he was in intensive care for several days.

With him in ICU was a young boy who had been hit by a car while riding his bicycle. He was seriously injured. Stuart was more worried about the little boy than himself. While sitting outside the unit, his mother and a friend came and sat down by me. I told them who I was and asked if we could pray together for her little boy. So we did. Several nights later, Jay, Lucy and I were visiting Stuart, and as we left, we saw a crowd outside the ICU. I knew the little boy was dying. I mentioned it to Lucy and Jay, but they didn't respond.

We were almost home and had stopped at a red light when the Holy Ghost came upon Jay. "We have to pray now for the little boy!" We did.

The next day, I inquired about the little boy. "Why he's been put in his own private room," I was told. I thanked the Lord for his mercy.

Stuart recovered during this hospital stay, and came home almost a new man. He had peace.

We had a palm tree in our front yard. In the past, when it needed trimming, he would come in with blood streaming down his arms from the branches. Now recuperating, there wasn't anything he could do, and he was restless. As he walked around the house, he looked out the kitchen window. He really didn't like that tree. He said, "If I could,

I would cut that tree down to the ground!" Seeing how scraggily it looked and there wasn't anything he could do about it, irritated him.

Time passed and we were low on finances. The cupboard was getting empty. I hesitated telling him but finally I said, "Honey we're getting low on groceries. We better pray." We prayed and asked the Lord for help."

A few days later, there was a knock on our front door. I answered, "Yes?"

It was a middle aged man whom I didn't know. "Excuse me, I am Mr. Roland. Do you own this house?"

"Yes?"

"I own a Palm Tree Nursery and I wonder if you would consider selling this tree to me?"

I struggled to keep a straight face. "I don't know. I'll have to ask my husband. Will you wait a minute?"

"Yes ma'am."

I shut the door and ran to the back of the house laughing. I told Stuart about the man at the front door.

"Will he dig it up and fill in the hole with dirt?" He answered seriously. He didn't see the humor in all this like I did. God has such a sense of humor sometimes, I think.

"I don't know. I'll ask him."

I asked Mr. Roland and he said he would. I asked how much he would pay for the tree. He told me and it was enough for a couple of weeks' groceries. Praise the Lord!

Mr. Roland came back to get the tree. While his crew was digging it up, I invited him in for a cup of coffee. As we talked, I asked him if he was a Christian. He said he was. Then I asked if he was a Spirit filled Christian. He got excited and said, "Yes!"

"Mr. Roland, let me share how God has used you in our lives."

I told him and we praised the Lord together.

Chapter 16

Going Home

We began praying for a church home near us. I felt like I had crossed a hot desert and needed building up and refreshing. One Sunday morning we attended a Spanish Church of God in a nearby town. We didn't speak or understand Spanish, but we recognized God's Holy Spirit when he was present.

There was a speaker from Teen Challenge that morning. We were familiar with Teen Challenge and were anticipating a wonderful worshipful experience. He preached in English as well as Spanish as a courtesy to us, since we were the only English speaking people present. God's presence blessed and it was like pouring cool water over parched souls.

After church the pastor asked how we came to be in the service that morning. He was pleased but said there was an English speaking, Church of God nearby in Baldwin Park which moved with God's Presence. He said Pastor Green was a godly man. We decided to visit that church and weren't disappointed. He was also right about the minister. He was a true, loving, "minister of the Lord."

Shortly after our visit to the church in Baldwin Park, two ladies came to our home for a visit. As we shared with each other, I inadvertently mentioned something about having a difficult spiritual situation in my home and that attracted the ear of one of the ladies. She decided to return so we could talk alone. She did and we became prayer partners and love each other to this day. She says we are spiritual twins. Her name is Carol.

She wanted to know about my experience living in the house. She knew about spiritual things like these, so I could speak without inhibition. Even more than that, the Lord began using us to minister. We would pray privately in our devotions for certain people and when the time was right, Carol generally knew when, we were to go and minister to them. We saw miracles and experienced great joy.

Meanwhile my home was "the place to go" for the children in the neighborhood. They knew they were welcome, and it was peaceful. One day Pastor Green visited. The kids were playing gospel music in the living room and talking and laughing. We found a semi-quiet place, so we could talk privately.

As Pastor Green was leaving, he paused and asked, "Don't you find it difficult being spiritual in these circumstances?"

I thought, *yes*, but said, "No, not at all" remembering what it was like before. I knew now wasn't the time to go into details. Besides, I didn't share with everyone about the history of my house, only if I felt the Lord leading me.

Stuart and I were feeling an inner nudge to move. We started looking around, but not too far from where we were living. We didn't see anything that appealed to us or anything which had the leading from the Lord. We weren't in a hurry so there wasn't any pressure.

I came home one day and found a sealed envelope over our telephone on the wall in the kitchen. I took it down and read the words written on the front. They were instructions to not open before six months had passed. Stuart had dated it.

I took the letter into the room where he was. "What is this?" I asked.

In his usual talkative way he answered, "What does it say?"

"Okay, now, what is happening? I can read, but what does this mean?"

"If it's God, it will come to pass. If it's not, then it won't!"

So I realized, he felt he had received something from the Lord. "I consider this is cruel and unusual punishment! Over the telephone! I'll have to stare at it every time I'm on the phone?"

Well, that was just the way it was.

When I was young, occasionally, I would meet someone who knew my biological father. Twice I was told my father wanted to see me when I was old enough.

Cynically I thought, how old is old enough? After all I was a teenager. I knew he was remarried and had a family. I didn't know if they knew about me or my mother. Consequently, I felt like I was in limbo concerning any relationship with him. I only remembered being with him once in my life when I was five years old. Now that I was saved, I felt I needed to meet that side of my family and share with them the things I was experiencing and learning about God. Since I was in California, and they were in Savannah, Georgia, I knew meeting them was out of the question.

One day I decided to put my family's name on a slip of paper and put it in the wooden prayer box on the altar in front of the sanctuary. People prayed over the box without disturbing or reading the requests. Prayerfully I dropped my little paper in the box. Then I forgot about it.

I was thinking about my mother one day and wrote her a letter thanking her for being so consistent in my upbringing. She was stern and I resented it at that time, but I could see the benefit now.

After she read my letter, she tucked it in her purse. When she went to the store for groceries, she saw my father's mother, my Grandmother.

She and my mother lived in the same community for thirty years, but my mother had never seen my grandmother in all that time. My mother still looked the same, just a little older. My grandmother had always been fond of my mother and was disappointed when my parents divorced.

They greeted each other warmly. In their conversation my grandmother said: "Louise, I know George would like to speak with Tommie. How can he reach her?"

"Mrs. Hodges, Tommie's in California, but I just happen to have her address on this envelope. If you would like, you can have it."

"Thank you so much."

My mother gave her the letter. When my mother got home, she was nervous and called me.

"Tommie, I just did something, and I'm not sure what will come from it. I believe I have been led by the Holy Spirit for the first time in my life."She then told me what she had done. I assured her it would be fine and that people were praying for him to contact me. She was relieved.

One day as I was sitting in my kitchen, I felt impressed with the gift of *knowledge* by the Holy Spirit that we were to go back home to Savannah. I got excited and called out to Stuart who was in another room. "Honey! I believe we're going home!"

"You can open the envelope now!"

"I don't need to. We're going home!" I never opened the envelope.

Soon I received a typewritten letter from my biological father and his wife, to whom he dictated the letter. He said he wanted to hear from me. He and his wife of over twenty years with whom he had his other children had divorced, and he had remarried. He and his current wife lived in Columbia, South Carolina.

I was excited and thanked God for the answered prayers. I called him right away, and he invited us to come for a visit. He said he wanted us to fly, and would pay all expenses.

I answered his letter and told him about my life. I told him what God had done for me, and when he received it, he made copies and sent them to all four of his other children. By this time, we realized we were to go back south, not to live in Savannah, but Columbia, South Carolina.

We put our house up for sale and began packing. The weekend we advertised it for sale, the night before the showing, there was a bad storm and the roof blew off the house. I was so disappointed and puzzled, why would this happen if it was the Lord's will we sell the house? A little doubt began to fester, but soon diminished when I learned we would get a much needed new roof. It was a good selling point and the insurance company would pay for it.

After about eight weeks, we sold the house and began the long journey back home. This time it was easier.

When we arrived at my parents home in Savannah, Georgia, as they hugged me in their kitchen, I felt the Holy Spirit's presence hover over us so strong, I wept. It was like, the Lord was saying to me, "See, I brought you back home to your mother and father."

I had a wonderful step-father. He didn't want me to move to South Carolina. He wanted us to live in Savannah near them. My mother knew the message I had to share, and that it was now time for me to know the other side of my family.

Now Mother told me she feared what had happened to her sister, Billie when she left for California might happen also to me. She also shared with me about the time when I was just three years old, I said to her, "One day I'm going far away and I'll miss you." Even though I was young, it penetrated her heart where she never forgot it. Mother told me she felt it was prophetical. She wasn't religious, but sensed this move was what I was talking about when it came to pass.

After a short visit with my family in Savannah, we continued on to West Columbia, South Carolina. We had made arrangements to meet at a filling station, since we didn't know our way around. Approaching the filling station, I could see the skyline of Columbia, and was amazed. What little I had seen of South Carolina near Savannah was very unimpressive. What a surprise. It was quite a large city; it is actually, the Capital of South Carolina.

We pulled into the filling station and didn't have long to wait. We got out of our cars, and I walked toward my father. Once again, I was surprised. I could see our resemblance. For the very first time, I saw from whom I inherited some of my features.

I had such strong emotions at that moment. It was like; I walked back over a long bridge to my childhood. I actually belonged to this stranger. He was my father and we embraced.

I didn't know what he was experiencing. Perhaps he shared with someone what this moment meant to him, but I believe it was very emotional for both of us. In some ways, it was awkward for me, and in other ways, I felt like a little girl that wanted to climb up into his lap and touch his face and say, "Daddy!" It didn't matter that I was thirty years old. It was a missing piece of the puzzle in my life finally put in its proper place. In these first moments, I was oblivious of my husband and our two children.

You and I have reached the end of this book, but not the end of the story. These are just the beginning years of my exciting life with Jesus.

"My God Makes House Calls!" "Shh, quiet! Listen! Can you hear?

He might be standing outside your door at this very moment. Can you hear Him knocking? Open the door and let Him in, and find peace, joy, and rest for your soul! Also, an extraordinary Savior will give you an extraordinary life."

Especially for you,

Nalley

Jesus is speaking: "Behold, I stand at the door, and knock: if any man hear my voice, and open the door, I will come in to him, and will sup with him, and he with me."[46]

---

46 Revelation 3:20

Afterword

"But the hour cometh, and now is, when the true worshippers shall worship the Father in spirit and in truth: for the Father seeketh such to worship him. God is a Spirit: and they that worship him must worship him in spirit and in truth." [47]

This is the experience Jesus explained to Nicodemas, a leader in Israel. The born again experience I speak so much about in my book is when a person becomes a Christian. You cannot be a Christian without this experience. This is the time when God places his Holy Spirit inside the human body of a Believer. Only God can perform this act on the person. [48]

If you have any doubt about your testimony of being a Christian, don't be alarmed or dismayed. God has promised to let you know personally that you are his child. It is written that the Holy Spirit himself will witness with our spirit that we are God's children. If the witness of man is great, how much greater is the witness that comes from God? [49] [50]

Christ will be inside of your body enabling you to live a life which pleases him. Everything necessary for a godly life will be available. This is the same Spirit who filled the Followers of Jesus in the upper room.

---

47 John 4:24
48 John 3:1–8
49 Romans 8:16
50 1 John 5:9–10

Then the Holy Spirit will gift you as it pleases him, empowering you with the ability to do the work you are called to do. [51]

When Jesus was instructing his disciples about the Holy Spirit, prior to the time he went to Gethsemane for prayer, he told them that the prince of the world was coming so he wouldn't speak further. This coming prince didn't have a hold on him, he said. When we read further and see Judas, possessed by Satan, leading those who were to arrest or lay hold on Jesus. I believe Jesus was reinforcing the fact that no man would take his life, but he was willingly laying it down as a sacrifice.

Moving on to the crucifixion, after the spiritual work was performed, Jesus said, "It is finished." Jesus then commended his spirit into the Father's hands. At this time, the earth shook, rocks were broken, the curtain (Vail) in the temple which hung between the Holy Place and the Holy of Holies was rent (torn) in two pieces breaking down the partition meant to separate. This is significant in that, only the priest had limited access into those two places, especially the Holy of Holies, in behalf of the people. The priest was set aside to represent the people before God. The scripture came in to play, "For there is one God, and one mediator between God and men, the man Christ Jesus; who gave himself a ransom for all, to be testified in due time." [52]

I believe during that time a war took place in heaven between Michael and his angels and the devil and his angels. The devil and his angels lost. They were thrown out of heaven and Satan couldn't appear before God anymore nor accuse the Brethren. Good news except that they were cast down to the earth. The devil was exceedingly angry, and he knew his time was short. Where is he going to expel that hatred? Yes, he's going to come against the followers of Jesus Christ!

At this same time, a loud proclamation was made in heaven which said, "*Now*(at this time) is come *salvation*, and *strength*, and *the kingdom of our* God, and *the power of his Chr*ist: for the accuser of our brethren is cast down, which accused them before our God day and night."[53]

---

51 Romans 8:9–12

  1 Corinthians 12: 1–11

  1 Corinthians 13, 14

52 1 Timothy 2:5–6

53 Revelation 12:7–12

Heaven and those who live there are rejoicing, but woe (great grief) to the earth and sea because the prince of the world is here with us in the world. God's plan is slowly unfolding.

Believers who are filled with the Holy Spirit are prepared with power from above. We have weapons, armor, and we overcome Satan by the blood of the Lamb (Jesus' sacrifice on the cross) and by the word of our testimony. [54] [55]

I realize this is history and one might be thinking what does this have to do with me or Christians today? The battle is not over. It is still raging; in fact, building in intensity. If the recognition of spiritual warfare hasn't increased since my encounters you read about in my book, we are lacking much knowledge in the religious world to instruct people when they encounter the enemy of Christ.

Why is this important to us in these modern days? We have been seductively influenced through every medium including radio, television, movies and literature. Satan has introduced new ways of thinking by introducing them as fiction or even comedy to; draw us into accepting these new ways as normal entertainment and behavior. At the same time, coming from other obscure directions, intimating that those who reject these new ideas as bigoted or narrow minded. Some recent books have not only been accepted and in great demand by our children, but also by many parents. It was revealed on television recently many children are suddenly experiencing paranormal gifts. I believe the appetite for spiritual experiences infiltrating our culture is the result of exposure to concentrated efforts of satanic influence which is producing spiritual fruit in their lives which needs its roots investigated.

To you who are born of the Holy Spirit, I would encourage you to test the spirits to be certain they are of God. Spirits who want to be "guides" are flooding our world today. Test them before you put your trust in them. Many are being deceived. [56]

I believe in my heart, I have obeyed the Lord by writing this book. I have prayed and continue to pray, it will help others who might be in

---

54 Ephesians 6:11–18
55 Revelation 12:11
56 1 John 4:1

similar situations. The Bible says, "Greater is he that is in you than he that is in the world."

Our heavenly Father is the Supreme Being. We are admonished to study to show ourselves approved unto God, a workman who needs not to be ashamed rightly dividing the word of truth. [57]

---

57 2 Timothy 2:15